The Dotted Red Line

The Dotted Red Line

Britain's Defence Policy in the Modern World

Jeremy Black

THE SOCIAL AFFAIRS UNIT

British Library Cataloguing in Publication Data
A catalogue record of this book is available from the British Library

Printed and bound in the United Kingdom

ISBN 1-904863-13-2

Social Affairs Unit
314-322 Regent Street
London W1B 5SA
www.socialaffairsunit.org.uk

FOR PETER AND JULIA LUFF

CONTENTS

PREFACE AND ACKNOWLEDGEMENTS

This book aims to provide a concise study of the key defence issues as they affect modern Britain. They will be located clearly in their relevant contexts, particularly foreign policy, but also in fiscal matters, and social and cultural trends. The focus is on recent history, current problems and probable trends, and the perspective is pragmatic and prudential. It has proved especially instructive to move from writing about war at the general level to considering the problems of a particular country.

I have benefited from the comments of General Lord David Ramsbotham on an earlier version and George Boyce on part of an earlier version.

Invitations to speak at the Australian Defence Force Academy, the Australian Land Warfare Centre, the Foreign Policy Research Institute, and Hawaii Pacific University have presented a very welcome opportunity to develop some of the ideas contained here.

I am grateful to Michael Mosbacher for asking me to write this book, and to Clive Liddiard for his helpful editing.

It is a great pleasure to dedicate this book to a university contemporary who, as well as being a public figure, is a very good fellow, and to his charming wife.

HISTORICAL NOTE

On 25 October 1854 the 93rd Highlanders, under the command of Sir Colin Campbell, faced the enemy at Balaclava. In his initial report of the battle, *The Times* correspondent W. H. Russell described how the Russian cavalry charged, gathering speed at every stride, and flew towards the 'thin red streak tipped with a line of steel'.

Although rapidly shortened in subsequent reports to the more familiar Thin Red *Line*, it was Robert Gibb's famous 1881 painting of that name that consolidated the phrase in the popular mind.

INTRODUCTION

Defence issues are important, but there is a tendency to treat defence and war as an adjunct to the major themes of post-1945 British history. This reflects two major trends: first, the degree to which basic social alignments and aspirations have indeed been governed by factors other than defence; and, second, the extent to which, for the British, war in this period has been largely a spectator activity.

It is certainly the case that Britain engaged in the military confrontation known as the 'Cold War' as a leading second-rank participant, if not *the* leading second-rank participant, contributing, for example, the second-biggest foreign contingent to the United Nations forces in the Korean War (1950–3). Furthermore, Britain had the second-largest navy in the Free World, and she also played a major role in a series of particular conflicts – first decolonization struggles, and then, from the Falklands War in 1982, various wars in response to the actions of other states that were disruptive of the international order, or at least the British interpretation of it: a process that culminated most recently in the invasion of Iraq in 2003.

Yet, in each case, the direct impact on the British home base seemed limited. In part, this was because the conflicts were not waged on British soil. Furthermore, the growing use of television reporting helped produce a spectator quality to the response of much of the public. This was bolstered by the end of conscription: not only did military service cease to be an experience shared by an entire cohort of young men, but its impact on partners, parents, neighbours and others was also weakened.

By contrast, there was no such retreat from public consciousness in the case of health, education, social welfare, law and order or economic policy. Indeed, the increased prominence of these issues in public anxiety and political contention led to militaristic vocabulary being used to describe them, rather than defence itself: there were wars on drugs, crime, poverty, etc. More subtly, the collectivism that had underpinned military service and social commitment during the two world wars slackened in the second half of the century, which was a period of increasing individualism, hedonism, and social atomization, both in personal behaviour and in the collective culture. All of these developments were antipathetic to military values. This was taken further by a cultural hostility to war that was evident, in particular, in the presentation of World War One. Books, plays, films and television programmes, such as *Oh! What a Lovely War*, *Gallipoli*, *Blackadder Goes Forth* and *The Monocled Mutineer*, presented generals as callous and incompetent. This was all an aspect of a more general tendency to mock patriotism that was fashionably radical in the 1960s, before becoming mainstream.

Given such social trends, political priorities and cultural patterns, it is not surprising that defence was displaced from public attention. Indeed, it is possible to read histories of the post-1945 period that consign it to a cul-de-sac, treating defence and the military largely as an offshoot of other issues, particularly decolonization, and focusing, for example, on the Campaign for Nuclear Disarmament – a movement that was, in fact, far less important than the development of the nuclear deterrent. The Falklands War of 1982 appears in such histories essentially in order to help explain Margaret Thatcher's electoral victory the following year, and it is likely that the Gulf War of 2003 will be mentioned largely in order to underline Tony Blair's mendacity.

This approach underrates the importance of the subject, as this book seeks to show. British defence policy and warfare in recent decades are not only instructive for military specialists, but are also significant as part of the account of the country and people. Furthermore, they raise important issues for policy consideration today – issues that relate directly to British foreign policy, and indeed to the sense of identity with which the latter sits in an uneasy relationship. This is a particular problem for the Conservative Party for a number of reasons. Traditionally, the Conservatives benefited electorally from their strong identification with defence and from their clarity about what it entailed. There was 'clear blue water' between Conservative views and the internationalism, criticism of the military, anti-war sympathies and indeed pacifism of much of the left. This became more pronounced when Labour lurched leftwards, becoming the party of Michael Foot rather than Major Attlee.

The situation was made more complex when Labour, particularly under Blair, altered its defence policy, and thus undermined the Conservative distinctiveness. Unilateral nuclear disarmament, for example, was ditched. This reorientation was taken further after Labour gained power in 1997, when Blair started to show a marked readiness to use force. The resulting conflicts left the Conservatives seriously wrong-footed. Their general reluctance to criticize national military initiatives – for fear of being, or appearing, unpatriotic – was matched by an unwillingness to oppose specific policies and conflicts. This was seen, in particular, during and after the Gulf War of 2003, and again in the large-scale Afghan deployment of 2006.

Furthermore, on the general question of the structure of the armed forces, the Conservatives found it easier to oppose cuts, and to press for increased expenditure, than to offer a coherent and sensibly costed programme. This was bound up with the difficulty they had in defining a clear set of national interests and priorities: a difficulty that was related to a lack of clarity in Conservative views on foreign policy. Clearly, these issues are the proper subjects of debate and contention, and what follows will not please all readers. However, this book will work if it elicits a critical response and helps the reader define and express his own views, including in opposition to what is written here. Writers are not magicians, able to unlock past, present and future, but guides who stimulate readers to see with their own eyes.

As a historian, it is useful for me to begin with a long-term perspective, for the distinctive Tory approach to defence began in the early days of the Tory party in England, at the close of the seventeenth century and in the opening decades of the eighteenth. Furthermore, defence and foreign policy were not then on the margins of party positions, but indeed were central to them. The Tory position was based on hostility to the continental interventionism associated with the rival Whigs; instead, the Tories counselled caution over foreign commitments, and particularly alliance politics and warfare on the European continent. As is always the case, in practice there was, in the formulation and expression of attitudes, a complex and not entirely comfortable interaction of short-term exigencies and opportunities with longer-term developments. As far as the latter were concerned, the Tory approach rested on a hostility to the development of central government after the 'Glorious Revolution' of 1688–9 and, specifically, to an increase in the size of the army to facilitate continental interventionism, which was seen by Tories as politically dangerous. In his influential pamphlet *The Conduct of the Allies* (1711), Jonathan Swift, a key Tory writer, complained that the very alliance system ensured that the purpose and conduct of the war was wrong:

> *First* That against all manner of prudence or common reason, we engaged in this war as principals, when we ought to have acted only as auxiliaries.
> *Secondly* That we spent all our vigour in pursuing that part of the war which could least answer the end we proposed by beginning of it; and made no efforts at all where we could have most weakened the common enemy, and at the same time enriched ourselves.
> *Lastly* That we suffered each of our allies to break every article in those treaties and agreements by which they were bound, and to lay the burden upon us.

Instead, the Tories focused on a 'blue water' policy: an expansion of naval strength, and its use in the unilateral pursuit of national interests, and particularly in pursuit of maritime hegemony and colonial gains outside Europe. Consequently, for example, in 1711, during the War of the

Spanish Succession, the Tory ministry of 1710–14 made a major, though ultimately unsuccessful, attempt to capture Québec, while the Whig emphasis had been on the war with France in the Low Countries.

This contrast remained throughout the years of Whig–Tory rivalry in the reigns of George I (1714–27) and George II (1727–60). Thereafter, however, the atomization of parties, which was greatly facilitated by the accession of George III (1760–1820), meant an end to the clear-cut Whig–Tory divide of earlier decades. War with first Revolutionary and then Napoleonic France (1793–1802, 1803–14, 1815), however, led anew to marked, albeit different, political and ideological divisions over foreign policy. The Tories were now clearly associated with war on France, in part as a reaction against its radical domestic agenda. There were, however, serious differences over what this war meant in practice, not least in terms of alliance politics and military planning, and specifically whether to focus on continental (European) or 'blue water' operations. In some respects, these differences represented an aspect of the commitments and problems of government; in others, a consequence of longstanding divisions within the conservative tradition.

This looked forward to the response to Germany in the first half of the twentieth century. Differences then again focused on alliance commitments and strategic planning, not least the extent to which it was possible to maintain a policy of indirect engagement, rather than, as in World War One, confronting the enemy in the main theatre. Differences over goal and method came to play a particularly disruptive role for the Conservatives at the time of appeasement in the 1930s. The policy of appeasing dictators – particularly, but not exclusively, Hitler – with which Neville Chamberlain was to be associated, was, in practice, not a coherent policy, still less an ideology, but the sum of a diverse set of responses to very varying problems. These responses were advanced on often very different grounds. Nevertheless, in large part appeasement rested on the belief that it was possible to reach settlements with dictators. In some respects, however, the very process of establishing goals and priorities, and of reaching a compromise both with the views of other powers and with the apparent limitations of British resources – a process that was continuous in foreign, imperial and military policy – could, at particular junctures and from a hostile perspective, be described in terms of appeasement. Furthermore, Chamberlain's was not the first government to be criticized for appeasing foreign powers. At the time of the first Falkland Islands crisis, in 1770–1, the ministry of Lord North, which was very much a conservative government, was attacked by William Pitt the Elder for 'supine neglect or wicked treachery'. In response, Dr Samuel Johnson, in his pro-government pamphlet *Thoughts on the Late Transactions Respecting Falkland's Islands* (1771), attacked Pitt's 'gabble'. Like other Tory commentators, however, he faced the problem of advocating a prudential policy: one that urged caution and a balanced assessment of risks and opportunities. This was linked to the traditional Tory refrain about the unpredictability and volatility of human affairs, and thus the centrality of uncertainty or, in modern terms, risk:

> It seems to be almost the universal error of historians to suppose it politically, as it is physically true, that every effect has a proportionate cause. In the inanimate action of matter upon matter, the motion produced can be but equal to the force of the moving power; but the operations of life, whether private or public, admit no such laws. The caprices of voluntary agents laugh at calculation. It is not always that there is a strong reason for a great event. Obstinacy and flexibility, malignity and kindness, give place alternately to each other.

Aside from criticism of appeasement, human rights and the often impassioned concern for the rights and interests of foreign peoples were inventions neither of the twentieth century, nor of the age of Blair. For example, in the 1870s, the Bulgarian massacres were used by Gladstone to attack the pro-Turkish policies of the Disraeli government.

The legacy of the debacle of appeasement was, thereafter, to condition, if not dictate, Conservative defence assumptions, as well as those of an important strain of Labour thought. The politics of prudence associated with appeasement was discredited and, instead, the Churchillian ethos prevailed; the Churchill, that is, of 1940, rather than of the earlier unsuccessful intervention in the Russian Civil War that had, in practice, highlighted the potential limitations of such a policy.

These assumptions appeared to be confirmed by the political alignment of defence during the Cold War. As the most anti-Communist of the leading political parties, it was understandable that the Conservatives should be the most robust in their commitment to the Western defence system. The creation of NATO might have been negotiated by a Labour government, but the Conservatives were scarcely going to reject it. This led to an underestimation of the extent to which NATO was a defensive system, rather than one committed to 'rollback'. Indeed, appeasement was as much in evidence over Hungary in 1956 and Czechoslovakia in 1968, as over Austria and Czechoslovakia in 1938. Looked at differently, the exigencies of power were such that commitments were framed, and responses developed, in terms not of a lasting strategic guideline, but rather of the opportunities and problems of the moment; opportunities and problems that were not clearly established by this guideline. The Falklands War of 1982 exemplified this, just as it also contributed to the culture of assumptions – particularly Conservative assumptions – by underlining the value of a robust response, as well as the possibility of fighting a war that had singularly few domestic disadvantages.

Politicians and commentators sought to confer a sense of morality and consistency on such choices, and, in the case of both Conservatives and Labour, found a ready audience and resonance in terms of powerful assumptions. It is difficult for members of both these parties to appreciate that these assumptions are not always particularly helpful in making careful and critical observations upon the unexpected tide of events. In the case of the Conservatives, their views have often overlapped directly with those of defence professionals. Indeed, after both world wars, a sizeable percentage of the parliamentary party was made up of former officers, and they played a major role in party defence policy. The problem with this approach is that the professionals, while well placed to advise on the capabilities of military means and the feasibility of goals, are far less able to comment on the desirability of the latter. Indeed, within the world of military professionals, an instinctive traditionalism can make debate unwelcome, while the focus on loyalty and obedience ensures that a hard-headed, critical evaluation of goals in public is not always possible. Indeed, the opposite is the case. The same is true of much of the traditional core of British Conservatism. Notions of appropriate military goals are embedded in a set of assumptions about national interests that have not, in most cases, critically adjusted to the shifts of policy over the last decade and a half. This is despite the extent to which the military itself has adapted greatly in a significant process of transformation. Driving this process, major changes in the intensity of interventionism have occurred under the Blair government.

If to oppose in order to seek to influence policy choices and presentation is one of the requirements of opposition, then this requirement was badly mishandled by the Conservatives in the early 2000s in the case of foreign policy and defence. It would be all too easy to blame this on the maladroit position of Iain Duncan Smith during the Iraq crisis, and indeed there was a serious failure to oblige the government to define its policy in terms of a carefully conceived and cogently presented assessment of both national interests and military practicalities. In practice, however, there was a more persistent and systematic misjudgement of the consequences of mission creep and moralism under Blair.

Looking ahead, it is unclear whether the current situation is sustainable, not least given Macmillan's remark about the challenges posed by 'events, dear boy, events'. This is most pronounced in the case of unsuccessful force projection. It is hardly necessary to mention Suez or Vietnam to underline the extent to which such projection can be unsuccessful. Lack of success may be defined not only in terms of serious difficulties (or even defeat) abroad, but also with reference to domestic dissension. In 2003, there was no serious political trouble over the Iraq crisis – either in terms of large-scale public disorder, or of awkward ministerial or parliamentary politics. It is far less clear that this will be the case in the future. Indeed, unfortunately, the contrast between the futility of peacetime protest in Britain in 2003 and the impact, at least in terms of attention, of the nihilistic terrorist violence of 2005 in London will suggest to some that violence can be of greater effect. Similar conclusions could be drawn from the French riots of 2005. Large-scale violence at home, be it of a terrorist or public disorder nature, is another instance of events that could well sap public support for current policy.

If events can thus shape the political parameters, it is also possible that financial factors will make strategy obsolescent because unaffordable. This is a situation that neither political party has adequately addressed. Government policy assumes a tri-service expeditionary force capable of acting at a significant operational level; but the cost of military systems is making that implausible in the medium term, just as it has successively closed off other options since World War Two. The capability outlined by the 1998 *Strategic Defence Review* and the 2002 *New Chapter* called for such a force, and for it to have the range to fulfil ambitious goals. But rising unit costs make this improbable if the force is intended to be 'state of the art'. The fascination with 'force multipliers' that underpins the modern cult of revolutionary technology in the shape of the RMA (Revolution in Military Affairs), NEC (Network Enabled Capability) and other acronyms does not adequately address the cost–capability issue. Instead, these beliefs represent an attempt to overcome the issue; an attempt, moreover, that raises not only the problem of additional costs, but also the prospect of finding that requirements do not match capabilities when the ability to cope with eventualities has been reduced by repeated cuts.

The historical context helps provide contrasts, as well as comparisons. This is clear, for example, in the interconnectedness of internal and external defence, which might be termed homeland security and power projection. When dealing with the IRA and the lesser threat of the Loyalist terrorists, there was no need to think in this way. There were IRA attacks on the continent, but countering them (in so far as any European government did so) was not Britain's responsibility – apart from tightening up security at British bases in Europe. Intervention in Bosnia, Kosovo and elsewhere raised no issues of British internal security. Now, in contrast, the homeland and external threats appear inseparable. This requires some rethinking of defence policy, but the government simply makes do and mends.

CHAPTER 1

THE LEGACY

The concept of strategic culture is as crucial to understanding the background to defence policy as it is to following military history. Focusing on 'tasking', or the setting of goals, directs attention to a demand-led account of policy. This is the reverse of the supply-side approach, which focuses rather on military capability, particularly technology, and its impact on warfare. While a demand-led account does not rule out a role for the consequences of technology and technological change in military development, the emphasis is, instead, on the limited efficiency of arms technologies and their dependence on what they are expected to achieve. In this demand-led account of military change, fitness for purpose – a key concept in weaponry, force structure and capability – is the major issue for evaluation, and the purpose of the military is set, not by the capability, but by the task required. This is very much a case of warfare as politics by other means. Military development is seen to lie less in what the military could achieve than in what they are required to undertake.

Tasks, however, attract only slight attention in popular discussion of warfare, as it appears self-evident that the task is victory – generally defined as total victory – and therefore that the best-prepared military wins. Such an approach to war owes much to the continual reiterations of World War Two as the prime instance of modern warfare. This, though, is an account of warfare that is of only limited relevance. First, the very nature of victory is dependent on the purpose of the military and its particular objectives, and thus on the process of tasking: whether, for example, to drive Iraqi forces from Kuwait, as in 1991, or both to conquer Iraq and then to overcome insurgency, as from 2003. Secondly, this process of tasking helps address the issue of prioritizing conflicting requirements, in terms not only of goals but also of related preparedness, ranging from equipment to doctrine. Thirdly, defining tasking and capability in terms of victory is unhelpful as, for most of the time, there is no conflict, and so it is necessary to consider how best to evaluate goals and effectiveness in scenarios of non- or near-war.

The strategic cultures within which goals are defined are far from immutable. In part, this is because the political assumptions and discussions that are crucial to strategic culture are far from fixed and are often difficult to disentangle. Furthermore, they are not in a simple causal relationship with the military. Instead, these assumptions and discussions are affected by military developments, including new weaponry, as well as by shifting geopolitical constructs. The latter respond to changes in political conceptions and alliance politics.

The concept of strategic culture overlaps with that of strategic landscapes, and has to address the contested character of national interests and thus the issue of who is defining the strategic culture. In addition, there is the question of the strategic culture of individual military services, and thus of competing strategic cultures. More than technology, geography and security interests are involved in assessing strategic culture. Attitudes to the appropriate nature and use of power also play a major role, and these reflect the potent legacy of the past. As an example of this, and of the variety of strategic cultures, several decades after the end of its empire Britain continues to place much emphasis on 'out-of-area' operations, whereas China has hitherto developed little capability to wage wars far from its own territory, although this may be changing with its growing interest in naval power.

Strategic culture is not only a matter of the response to the wider world. There is also the question of the domestic scenario, including the type of command and the nature of recruitment. Civilian control is a key element of the British military legacy and is fundamental to defence policy; it is so much of a given that it tends not to be mentioned. This control was maintained during the twentieth century. In World War

One there was much tension as Lloyd George sought to impose control on the generals, although there was much about his 'control' that was dubious in military terms. In World War Two, there was far less tension, in large part because the generals were under control. In neither war did British leaders need to bribe some generals with land and money, and execute others, as Hitler did.

This situation did not change thereafter. Unlike in France and (very differently) Portugal, de-colonization led to no serious differences between politicians and the military, let alone coup attempts. The quarrels in Britain over force structures and military commitments were contained before they flared into sustained disputes, let alone military pressure on the political world, which largely operated as if the military did not have an independent role. The cancellation in 1966 of the CVA-01, a large planned fleet carrier, led to the resignation of both the minister for the navy and the Chief of the Naval Staff, but the dispute went no further. Military uncertainty about the decision to attack Iraq in 2003 did not lead to public criticism by senior serving commanders, although their retired counterparts were more critical. Furthermore, unlike in Germany and Italy in the twentieth century, ex-servicemen's organizations did not become a political force. The military did not interfere in civilian politics, even in periods of real or apparent crisis such as 1973–4 and 1975–6. Had Thatcher been forced to back down in the face of the miners' strike of 1984–5, the military would not have intervened. Moreover, a major effort was made by the military to adopt norms similar to those prevailing in society. Thus the officer ranks are now far less dominated by the upper class than a century ago, while recruitment from ethnic minorities has been encouraged and there has been a greater willingness to accept technical values.

The traditional dichotomy in British strategic culture corresponded with a marked tension within foreign policy. It focused on the debate between the direct and indirect approach, which was linked to that between continental interventionism and the 'blue water' policy of standing back from the European continent and focusing rather on naval strength and transoceanic interests. This tension can be traced back through British history and emerges as the central issue in strategic thought, and thus in debates over military goals and force structure. The Oxford historian R. B. Wernham, indeed, argued in 1980 that 'there was built into English foreign policy a duality of ocean and continent. In normal, peaceful times the dominant influence, the dominant attraction was that of the ocean. In times of European crisis, the influence of the continent was the more powerful.'[1]

As the British state consolidated and became more powerful, it required a multiple military capability. Military power rested on four fundamental capabilities: the successful suppression of internal revolt (except in North America in 1775–83); a small but generally effective army that could engage its larger enemies in Europe; naval dominance; and successful transoceanic land warfare. Capability and policy options were also linked with the attitude of other states. In 1901, the 2nd Earl of Selborne, the First Lord of the Admiralty in the Conservative government, observed:

> I would not quarrel with the United States if I could possibly avoid it...[I]f the Americans chose to pay for what they can easily afford, they can gradually build up a navy firstly as large and then larger than ours and I am not sure they will not do it.[2]

The British were indeed fortunate to find the USA, eventually, their ally in both world wars; and in each case, before American entry, Britain was able to take advantage of the strength of the American economy, thanks to British naval dominance of the Atlantic and creditworthiness. American support underlined the extent to which British warmaking depended on multiple alliance systems. At the most basic level, this meant cooperation between the parts of the United Kingdom, and, secondly, within the empire, the latter proving particularly important to the struggle in the Atlantic and in north-west Europe (Canada), and in Mediterranean, Middle Eastern and Asian operations (India, Australia, New Zealand). Lastly, there was the crucial nature of formal alliances with other powers, particularly the USA, but also, in World War Two, the Soviet Union.

All of these levels of cooperation were to be put under strain, even that within the United Kingdom, where much of Ireland gained independence after World War One. Cooperation with the USA in the defence of Western Europe and the North Atlantic through NATO from 1949 helped maintain the international level of cooperation but, after World War Two, decolonization and greater Dominion autonomy ensured that Britain could bring less to the strategic table. Indian independence in 1947 was particularly important, as Indian troops had been crucial to Britain's expeditionary capacity in Asia, Africa and the Middle East. The loss of these troops removed an important mainstay of the British Empire's military dimension: for example, in 1941, Indian forces had played a major role in the successful invasion of Iraq, but just a decade later, when Britain was in dispute with the nationalist government in Iran over its seizure of Britain's oil interests, Plan Y, the plan for military intervention involving the seizure of Abadan, was not pursued, largely because, without Indian troops and with British forces committed in Germany and Korea, it no longer seemed militarily viable. There were no Indian troops to help in the attack on Egypt in 1956, or to enable Britain to participate in the Vietnam War, had that been a goal. And Britain was only able to intervene in the two Gulf wars as a junior ally of the USA. By then, any notion of Britain deploying Indian troops was but a distant memory.

Assertiveness in the 1950s, particularly in Malaya and Kenya, at Suez and in Cyprus, and in British membership of the South-East Asia Treaty Organization (SEATO) and the Baghdad Pact, was intended to protect British interests and to demonstrate that Britain was not weak. However, these commitments put serious pressure on Britain's ability to maintain force levels in Europe as part of NATO – a strategic goal that itself, in turn, compromised Britain's role as a military power outside Europe. As part of the NATO commitment, Britain had to defend a section of the West German frontier.

The Suez Crisis of 1956 saw a major display of British

military power, but American opposition, which underlined the vulnerability of the British economy, was crucial in weakening British resolve and led to a humiliating withdrawal. The Suez Crisis, indeed, marked the end of Britain's resolve to act independently; from then on, there was an implicit reliance on American acceptance, as in the Falklands War in 1982. Furthermore, the pace of decolonization dramatically increased after Suez. This was largely due to a shift in attitude within the Conservative government, but defence factors did play a role. Colonies now appeared less necessary in defence terms; not only because of alliance with the USA, but also because, in 1957, Britain had augmented the atomic bomb with a hydrogen device.

Military deployments, nevertheless, continued in the defence and protection of formal and informal empire – particularly in Jordan (1958), Kuwait (1961), Brunei (1962), Malaysia (1963–6), Aden (1963–7), East Africa (1964) and Anguilla (1969) – and this was related to an ambitious sense of British power, one that was in no way restricted to NATO roles. Harold Wilson, who became Labour prime minister in 1964 (and who prefigured Blair in a number of respects, not least commitment to modernization, showmanship, and willingness to regulate the trade unions), hoped to maintain Britain's role as a major independent power, and sought to act as a leading figure on the international stage. In support of India against China, and reflecting serious concern over the consequences of China's easy victory over India in the brief border war of 1962, Wilson declared that 'Britain's frontiers are on the Himalayas'. The possibility that China would follow up its victory appeared to threaten the stability of the Indian Ocean rim and, with it, Britain's interests in South-West and South-East Asia. British strategic thinking, which owed much to the geopolitical ideas of Halford Mackinder, discerned a tension between the Eurasian heartland and the oceanic rim, and thus saw the stability of South Asia and the Indian Ocean as closely linked. In this conception, Britain could play a key role if it could project its power in that ocean. As the Persian Gulf is an extension of the Indian Ocean, this strategic assumption looked forward to subsequent British roles. The political context was to change, but the geopolitical context remained far more stable.

In 1960, the carrier *Victorious* had joined the Far East station with several nuclear bombs aboard, and with the planes able to drop them. Subsequent war planning called for the use of a carrier able to mount nuclear strikes on southern China, and for a second carrier to be deployed in 1964. These carriers were to complement RAF planes based in Singapore. Indeed, when Wilson came to power in 1964, Britain had more troops 'east of Suez' than in Germany, and he initially maintained that commitment. The British presence in the Indian Ocean was anchored with bases in Aden and Singapore. Planning for the new submarines – armed with Polaris missiles with nuclear warheads – included having firing stations in the Indian Ocean designed both to block the Himalayan passes through which the Chinese could advance on India, and to reach targets in the southern Soviet Union.

However, this military capability was out of kilter with Britain's underlying position. The attempt to act as an independent power failed. Britain lacked the necessary diplomatic strength to further its goals, let alone help settle disputes or conflicts in Southern Rhodesia and Vietnam, and between India and Pakistan. Severe financial problems also hit hard. These led to a major devaluation of sterling in 1967 after a protracted attempt to defend it. This was a savage humiliation, and an important symbolic loss of international fiscal power. As a result, under pressure from the Chiefs of Staff, who were concerned about the mismatch between commitments and resources, in January 1968 the government announced that it was abandoning Britain's military position 'east of Suez', and forces were withdrawn from the Persian Gulf in 1971 and, largely, from Singapore the same year. This was a major shift in British strategic culture, and one that greatly attenuated military links with Australasia. The changes were important aspects of a more general shift, in which the USA occupied Britain's strategic position in the Indian Ocean and Persian Gulf. Edward Heath, who became Conservative prime minister in 1970, maintained the policy of withdrawal.

Furthermore, the British military from the 1960s became more clearly dependent on American weaponry. This was the case with the Polaris missile and its eventual replacement, Trident, and also with the decision in 1965 to purchase the F-111 jet in order to fill the gap after the cancellation of the projected British TSR-2 strike-reconnaissance plane, which was late and over budget. The purchase of the F-111, in turn, was cancelled in 1968, following a further British defence review – which in fact signalled a retrenchment of forces in the light of serious fiscal exigencies.

In December 1962, in what became known as the Nassau Agreement, Macmillan and Kennedy had decided that the Americans would provide Polaris for a class of four British nuclear-powered submarines that were to be built, although American agreement was dependent on the British force being primarily allocated to NATO duties, an important indicator of the strategic relationship. Indeed, British strategic interests were increasingly focused in the NATO area. This can be seen as the military equivalent to membership of the European Economic Community (EEC), which became a government priority from the early 1960s for both Labour and Conservative, and was finally achieved in 1973. Yet the processes, although related at the level of strategic culture, were different. The EEC was seen as a way to anchor Western Europe in the anti-Communist camp, but it was also deliberately constructed as a non-military alliance, as it was not intended to challenge NATO and its vital American link. At sea, a focus on the NATO area was a consequence of the build-up of the Soviet fleet from the 1950s, and much of the British fleet was allocated to the standing Naval Force Atlantic, a NATO force established in 1967. Multilateralism within NATO diminished the independent role of the British strategy, and this was taken further in 1966 with the cancellation of the planned CVA-01 carrier. This was an important aspect of a major series of defence cuts (which, in 1968, also saw the amalgamation of regiments) that reflected the economic problems, financial stringency and political priorities of the period.

It was envisaged that, after the existing aircraft carriers

with their distant strike capability were withdrawn from service, naval air power would amount essentially to helicopters designed to act against Soviet submarines in the Atlantic. An ability to support amphibious operations no longer seemed necessary – a major shift in military tasking. Indeed, the British forces were already in Western Europe, in the former occupation zone within West Germany, as the British Army of the Rhine, so that, in the event of conflict, there would be no need to move troops to the area; in contrast, in 1914 and 1939 it had been necessary to deploy troops from Britain to France. British defence priorities were focused on Western Europe and the North Atlantic. Forces were committed to these goals, the British being obliged to maintain 55,000 troops in Germany in order to man the 65 kilometres of the Inner German Border that Britain had to defend. If numbers were reduced, for example to assist with the situation in Northern Ireland, it was necessary to seek NATO permission and to promise to restore the agreed strength. The obligations were cross-service, as part of the RAF was located in West Germany. These priorities were not simply a matter of numbers, but also of capability; for the threat of attack by the USSR and the nature of its military obliged the British to upgrade in order to match Soviet improvements. The army as a whole was equipped and trained primarily for this task, with the strategic, operational and tactical emphasis on resisting heavily armed and more numerous attacking Soviet forces. Thus, the stress was placed on defensive fighting, not manoeuvre.

Within Western Europe, there was also an important revival in commitment to home defence, seen not in the shape of the defence of Britain against invasion, but rather in dealing with sustained civil unrest in Northern Ireland. Much of the army served there and, in terms of manpower and training, Northern Ireland became a major commitment. This underlined the variety of military tasks. In place of the focus on state-to-state conflict with regulars, as seen in NATO training, came support for the civil power function that had proved so important in the defence of empire. Indeed, the dispatch of reinforcements to Northern Ireland in 1969 followed swiftly on the heels of the withdrawal of forces from Aden after failure there. The need to succeed was more apparent in Northern Ireland, and the context of domestic political and public scrutiny was much more trying for both military and government. Despite the difficulties of the situation, the army, which increased its strength in Northern Ireland to 20,000 troops in 1972, succeeded in ending the 'no-go' areas that the Provisional IRA had created as a standard stage in the Maoist theory of revolutionary warfare. Confronting terrorism, however, proved a more arduous challenge, with the army having to maintain a semblance of order sufficient to demonstrate to the Catholic nationalist terrorists of the Provisional IRA that they could not win, and also to encourage intransigent politicians eventually to talk to each other. This proved a very long-term commitment, and one that was a major strain on manpower and morale. Nevertheless, the infantry, which bore most of the commitment, proved resilient, and training adjusted to the particular challenges of the task.

The commitment to Northern Ireland exemplified the degree to which it was inappropriate to prepare solely for industrial wars between industrial nations. Indeed, to a considerable extent, nuclear weaponry made such warfare unlikely. Instead, warfare among civilian populations was a common feature of the 'Cold War' period. It was inevitable that civilians would bear the brunt of any casualties inflicted if solely military action was taken against revolutionaries and/or terrorists based in their midst. This meant that there had to be question marks over Cold War weaponry, not least because of the horrendous lethality of modern battlefield weapons against any concentration of military force. Such lethality was inappropriate for the new style of anti-insurgency conflict, especially as political and diplomatic considerations came to the fore.

More generally, British strategic options seemed no longer to be those of independence or alliance from a position of strength, but instead to be those of centring political interests and defence undertakings on American or European systems. Although lessened by the role of NATO, the tension between

American and European alignments was to be the theme of British power politics thereafter. Roles and bases further afield diminished. In 1975–9, the Simonstown agreements with South Africa were terminated, forces were withdrawn from Singapore and Malta, SEATO was dissolved, and there was no pretence that Hong Kong could be defended if China chose to attack. Self-determination for Hong Kong was not an option. Gibraltar could be protected if necessary, but not Hong Kong. The last large, fixed-wing, strike aircraft carrier, *Ark Royal*, was decommissioned in 1978, the year in which *Eagle* was also broken up. They were to be replaced by a new type of carrier equipped with VSTOL[3] planes designed to act against submarines. A marked drawing in of commitments and concerns had taken place, and there seemed little prospect of anything else.

1 R. B. Wernham, *The Making of Elizabethan Foreign Policy, 1558–1603* (Berkeley, 1980), p. 95.
2 Selborne to Curzon, 19 April 1901; in D. G. Boyce (ed.), *The Crisis of British Power: The Imperial and Naval Papers of the Second Earl of Selborne, 1895–1910* (London, 1990), p. 115.
3 Vertical/Short Take-off and Landing.

CHAPTER 2

THE END OF THE COLD WAR

The Falklands War of 1982 underlined the unpredictability of military goals and responsibilities. The British military was not configured for such a conflict, and nor did the government anticipate it. Indeed, under Margaret Thatcher, who became Conservative prime minister in 1979, there was a strong focus on the Cold War. East–West tensions had revived markedly with the Soviet intervention in Afghanistan at the close of 1979, and the settlement of the Rhodesia question in 1980 further ensured a British focus on the Cold War. This was seen to involve a concentration on the defence of Western Europe, rather than on capability further afield, and it hit hard at the navalist legacy. In 1979, *Blake*, the last active cruiser, was decommissioned, while *Bulwark*, a 'commando carrier', was laid up in 1981. That year, the defence review, *The Way Forward*, implied that the navy was not concentrating on what should be its core mission, and suggested that there was an anachronistic emphasis on the surface fleet. Defence Secretary John Nott argued that Britain's NATO obligations to defend Western Europe had to come first, and had to determine force structure.

The Falklands War was to suggest otherwise. The archipelago had been under British control since 1833, but was claimed, as the Malvinas, by the Argentinians. Their navy had long sought to regain the Falklands in order to demonstrate its role in protecting the patrimony, and a desire to appease naval opinion finally prompted Argentina's military rulers to act. Back in 1976, after a military junta had seized power from the civilian government of Isabelita Peron, the navy had raised the Argentine flag on South Thule in the South Sandwich Islands. However, the following year, threatening Argentinian manoeuvres were countered by a British response that involved a task force of two frigates and a submarine. In December 1981, a new junta seized power in Argentina. Its naval member convinced the junta that the British government, uncertain of the desirability of retaining the colony, would accept its seizure. The decision, in 1981, to withdraw the Antarctic patrol ship *Endurance* was seen as a sign of Britain's lack of interest in the South Atlantic (and was indeed foolish), and, on 2 April 1982, Operation Rosario swung into action and the virtually undefended islands were successfully invaded. The British policy of prevarication had failed to satisfy or deter the Argentinians.

The subsequent conflict was important for the politics of both states, and also for the light it shone on British military capability in a particular context. Assured that the navy (which was anxious to assert its indispensability) could fulfil the task, and determined to act firmly in what was correctly seen as a make-or-break moment for the government, Thatcher decided to respond with Operation Corporate: an expeditionary force, dispatched on 5 April, that included most of the navy. In all, 51 ships were to take part in the operation. As another sign of British maritime strength, 68 ships were 'taken up from trade', contracted and requisitioned, including the cruise ships *Queen Elizabeth II* and *Canberra*, which were used to transport troops, and the container ship *Atlantic Conveyor*, which, in the event, was to be sunk by an Exocet missile, taking a large quantity of stores to the bottom. The speed with which the operation was mounted contrasted markedly with the time it had taken for the Suez expedition in 1956. The mismanagement of the latter had given time for hostile domestic and international opinion to be expressed more forcefully.

Both political and military preparedness were at issue for Britain. Politically, the government, which had not been prepared, benefited from an upsurge in domestic popularity. The Argentinian junta lacked a support base – despite nationalist graffiti in Northern Ireland praising the Argentinians, British Catholics did not play a role comparable to that of certain Moslems in the mid-2000s. Furthermore, the Labour Party leader, Michael Foot, badly misjudged the Conservative response. Thinking that this was another instance of Conservative appeasement, Foot pressed for action against the right-wing dictatorship (he was more tolerant of the left-wing variety), only to find Thatcher ready to provide it. As a result, it was Labour that was split; by contrast, there were very few Conservatives critical of the leadership. The failure before the conflict to provide deterrent signs to Argentina was not brought home to the government at this stage, and later enquiries were to lack political weight.

Internationally, the nature of the Argentinian junta and the fact that the Falkland islanders did not want to be ruled from Buenos Aires ensured that Britain benefited from a more supportive response than had been in evidence during the Suez crisis. American policy, however, proved rather awkward. On 29 March 1982, Sir Nicholas Henderson, the British envoy to Washington, responded to American pressure for restraint over South Georgia by wondering to what extent British neutrality would be appreciated if Puerto Rico were under attack.[1] Lord Carrington, the foreign secretary, told an American diplomat that Britain had supported American policy over Sinai and El Salvador without enthusiasm and against its better judgement, but out of solidarity with its closest ally, and that the government expected an appropriate American response. The Reagan administration, however, supported conservative Latin American regimes, such as that in Argentina, and was concerned that a defeated Argentina might go Communist. There was also no desire to see a war between two allies; and particularly not if that war risked having many of NATO's North Atlantic naval assets consigned to the bottom of the ocean. More generally, the American response was a reminder of the conditional nature of alliances and of the need, in response, to rely on resolve and to utilize divisions among policymakers. Indeed, the Falklands War showed the American administration to be very divided. The USA attempted mediation that would have left the Falklands under Argentinian control, but Thatcher rejected these efforts – sensibly so, as they would have weakened her domestically and left the Falkland islanders under rule by a military junta. Initially, the British found Mitterrand more ready to offer support, not least in the form of information on the Exocet missiles that had been sold by France. The recent claim by Mitterrand's psychoanalyst that Thatcher had threatened the use of nuclear weaponry against Argentina unless France provided this information seems implausible.

There was also the issue of military preparedness. As a result of the shift away from large fleet carriers (not least the cancellation of the CVA-01 project in 1966), the expeditionary force lacked a large aircraft carrier, and therefore airborne warning of attacks. It had, however, two smaller carriers. The light fleet carrier *Hermes*, which had been converted into a helicopter carrier in 1971–3, had, in 1980–1, been fitted with a ski-jump bow ramp to assist the take-off of Sea Harrier fighter-bomber VSTOL planes. The 16,000-ton *Invincible*, laid down in 1973 and commissioned in 1980, was the largest vessel built for the navy since 1945 and was also designed for Sea Harriers. By contrast, the Argentinian aircraft carrier, *25 de Mayo* – built in World War Two as HMS *Venerable* and sold to the Dutch in 1948, before being taken out of service by them in 1968 and sold to Argentina – had not been refitted to operate the Super Etendard aircraft Argentina had bought from France. As a result, it was unable to play a significant role in the war. Fortunately, the proposal by British Defence Sales to sell a carrier plus Harriers to Argentina had led nowhere.

On 25–26 April, the British recaptured the subsidiary territory of South Georgia and, on 1 May, large-scale hostilities began when the British tried bombing the runway of Port Stanley, the capital of the Falklands, to disable it. The following day, *Conqueror*, a nuclear-powered submarine, sank the Argentinian cruiser *General Belgrano*. This was crucial to the struggle for command of the sea, as it made the Argentinian navy desist from threatening attack. There was to be much contention over the sinking of the *Belgrano*, but, as its intention was clearly to threaten the British task force, failure to sink the ship would have been a serious neglect of responsibility.

Indeed, as a reminder of the vulnerability of the task force, air-launched Exocet missiles and bombs led to the loss of six British ships. Another eleven were damaged, while thirteen bombs hit ships but failed to explode. This showed that modern anti-aircraft missile systems, in this case Sea Dart and Sea Wolf, were not necessarily a match for manned aircraft and revealed a lack of adequate preparedness on the part of the navy, which had to rely on missile systems not hitherto tested in war. An Exocet was responsible for the loss of the destroyer *Sheffield* on 4 May, and bombs for the loss of the *Coventry* on 25 May. However, the Argentinians did not sink the two carriers that provided vital air support (but not superiority) for both sea and land operations. Designed for anti-submarine warfare in the North Atlantic, the carriers' Sea King helicopters and Harriers demonstrated their versatility. The Harriers did so both in combat air patrol, protecting the task force, and in close air support, attacking the Argentinians on the Falklands. The latter outnumbered the British force, and also had both aircraft and helicopters, while the British were short of ammunition because they had underestimated the requirements, and were operating at the end of a very long supply line. Nevertheless, after landing on 21 May, British troops advanced on Port Stanley, fighting some bitter engagements on the nearby hills and forcing the 11,400 isolated, demoralized and beaten Argentinians to surrender on 14 June.

American logistical and intelligence support had aided the British, particularly in the supply of 12.5 million gallons of highly refined aviation fuel and Sidewinder missiles, and in the use of satellite-based communications. Nevertheless, in the end, it was a matter of bravely executed attacks, good morale, the careful integration of infantry with artillery support, and the ability to continue without control of the air. The British were by no means assured of success merely by landing, for the Argentinian plan relied on fighting on from fixed positions, in order to wear down British numbers and supplies, and to take advantage of the onset of the bitter South Atlantic winter. It was British success in the field, combined with a continued ability to maintain the initiative, that destroyed the

Argentinians' will to fight. This was crucial, as they still had plentiful troops, artillery and supplies when they surrendered.

It would be easy to chart a course from the Falklands to the second Gulf War and the invasion of Iraq in 2003 by arguing that the trajectory of military activity focused on long-range force projection, and that the Falklands War revealed the need for amphibious capability and joint operations that were to become regular features of such activity. Linked to this approach would be a semi-automatic pattern of approbation or criticism of particular investments in weaponry and related policy initiatives based on the degree to which they conformed to this trajectory.

The Falklands War certainly revealed the value of preserving a balanced force structure, allowing Britain to take action on its own, rather than simply focusing on a number of specialized areas within an alliance division of labour. The latter approach, by contrast, is central to much of the current discussion, and there is an emphasis in particular on a capacity for integration within an American-directed structure. However, present plans do include provision of the capability to mount moderate-sized operations alone or with Britain playing the key role within the coalition. From that perspective, the option of a Falklands-style expedition has been retained, although the risk of defeat if the opponent is strong remains, as does the dependence on American acceptance. In the Falklands War, the nature of the war, although difficult, played into British hands, since the small local population was friendly and it was possible to isolate the Argentinian occupation force from Argentina. In that respect, the war offered scant guidance as to the likely nature and risks of modern expeditionary warfare.

To chart a course from the Falklands to the invasion of Iraq, however, ignores the indeterminacy of warfare. Furthermore, in the specific case of the 1980s, the Falklands led nowhere. After the war, the islands were developed, at considerable expense, as a military base, ensuring a new tri-service commitment; but the key event of the early 1980s was an upsurge in Cold War tension, much of it focused in Europe – an upsurge that encouraged a real growth in the defence budget.

Indeed, 1983 was a year in which confrontation came close to conflict. The deployment of cruise and Pershing missiles proved particularly sensitive. The shooting down, over Soviet airspace, of a Korean airliner suspected of espionage led to a marked increase in tension, as did Soviet fears of attack during a NATO exercise: the KGB provided inaccurate reports of American plans for a surprise nuclear first strike.

The risk of war posed major problems for the British military, as it would be in the forefront of resisting any Soviet attack. For the navy, there would be the challenge to North Atlantic routes and the need to block Soviet submarines, both in the Denmark Strait between Iceland and Greenland, and between Greenland and Britain. The Soviet naval challenge in the 1980s was accentuated, as six Typhoons, the largest ballistic-missile submarines ever built, entered service along with impressive surface warships, including the *Admiral Kuznetsov*, the only large Soviet carrier. For the RAF, there was the problem of protecting Britain and British forces in continental Europe, and in particular of providing a coherent air-defence system capable of intercepting long-range Soviet bombers. Furthermore, there was a need to take the war to the Soviets.

As far as the defence of Western Europe was concerned, from the mid-1970s there was a greater understanding of Soviet concepts of 'Deep Battle', which owed something to the work of the government-supported Soviet Studies Research Centre. The Soviets were a formidable force. Placing an emphasis on mobility and tempo, they planned a rapid advance into NATO rear areas, which would have compromised the use, in response, of Western nuclear weaponry. The Soviet emphasis on the offensive led to stress being laid on combined arms operations, with a major contribution from armour. In Soviet conventional operational methods, lead divisions were to attack until they were fought out, and were then to be replaced by second and third echelon forces, taking full advantage of their numerical superiority over their NATO foes, and thereby sustaining the tempo of the offensive. These Soviet ideas, which had been bolstered by the spread of mechanization in their army and by the growth of their airborne forces, led in response to the Western forces emphasizing their ability to mount a flexible defence, allowing them to regain, and exploit, the initiative.

In contrast to the Soviet emphasis on replacement, the less numerous Western forces depended on reconstitution, with individual units receiving replacements, and also battlefield repair and recovery, in order to sustain units in contact indefinitely. Faced with greater mass, the NATO forces also had the problem of resting on the defensive. Although the protection of West Germany led to the preparation of fixed defences, there was a clear need for mobility, and this led the British to emphasize their armour. Their position was underlined by lessons drawn from wars abroad. The Israeli victory against Egyptian and Syrian defensive positions in the Six Day War of 1967 and, eventually, after initial Egyptian and Syrian successes, in the Yom Kippur War of 1973, showed the value of mobility, and the vulnerability of forces with a low rate of activity. Greater British engagement with the manoeuvrist approach, which was called for in Richard Simpkin's *Race to the Swift: Thoughts on Warfare in the Twenty-First Century* (1985), owed much to the role of Sir Nigel Bagnall, successively commander of the 1st British Corps in Germany (1981–3) and of NATO's Northern Army Group (1983–5), and Chief of the General Staff from 1988. He pushed the manoeuvrist approach and the operational level hard.

Furthermore, the British had to be able to keep pace with the development of American doctrine, which, in turn, owed something to British analytical advances. The American doctrine of 'AirLand Battle', advanced in 1982, led to an emphasis on the integration of firepower with mobility in order to thwart Soviet Deep Battle. This involved not only flexibility in planning, with effective synergy between land and air, but also expensive investment in the modernization of conventional weaponry to achieve these goals. AirLand was designed to permit the engagement and destruction of the second and third-echelon Warsaw Pact forces, at the same time as the main ground battle was taking place along the front. Major developments in the capability of airpower were particularly important to AirLand. These included the advances stemming from more powerful aircraft-mounted radars; the enhancement of air combat resulting from heat-seeking short-range missiles and their radar-guided, long-range counterparts; and the use of AWACS (Airborne Warning and Control System) aircraft.

In the event, there was no war. Instead, there was a marked reduction in tension that stemmed from the rise to power in the Soviet Union, in 1985, of Mikhail Gorbachev, a leader committed to reform at home and good relations abroad. The action–reaction nature of NATO goals and capability were clearly demonstrated in the outcome. Designed to protect Western Europe, and not to 'roll back' Soviet control, NATO responded to Soviet passivity not by planning to exploit weakness, the fear voiced by the KGB, but by providing a context for the safe negotiation of a reduction in military tension. In 1987, the Soviet government accepted the Intermediate Nuclear Forces Treaty. By scrapping land-based missiles with ranges of between 500 and 5,000 kilometres, this forced heavier cuts on the Soviets and, at the same time, set up a system of verification through on-site inspection. Furthermore, in 1990, NATO and the Warsaw Pact were able to agree a limitation of conventional forces in Europe.

The absence of war in Europe in the 1980s means that it is difficult to judge British military capability and doctrinal advances then. The issue was no less serious just because, in any war with the Soviet Union, Britain would have been engaged as part of an alliance in which the USA was politically and militarily dominant. The absence of war also encouraged more wargaming in the field (or, increasingly nowadays, on screen) at all levels of military training and preparation, in order to evaluate might-have-beens. Such wargaming has become more necessary because of the greater infrequency of conflict, and also because of the rate at which new weapon systems are introduced and the range of possible military tasks. It is important to appreciate the degree to which might-have-beens provide much of the character of military evaluation. Had Gorbachev succeeded in pushing through reform

Communism, both in the Soviet Union and in Eastern Europe, then the consequences of a failure to exploit weakness in the late 1980s might be viewed in a very different light. The analogy with China appears clear in this context; but that analogy also indicates the difficulties of exerting military pressure short of actual conflict. Indeed, to return to Europe in the late 1980s, the earlier instances of Hungary (1956), Czechoslovakia (1968) and Poland (1981) all indicate the difficulties that NATO faced in influencing developments in Eastern Europe. Deterrence operated in both directions, and also affected political, as well as military, initiatives and thus capability. For the West, it was political initiative that was most useful in influencing developments in Eastern Europe. But this, again, could work both ways, as was shown by concern over the implications for NATO of West Germany's *Ostpolitik*. Thus, as an aspect of a multilateral system, British capability was affected by potential changes, such as German neutralism. Furthermore, American engagement in East Asia, particularly but not exclusively the Vietnam War, had seriously accentuated NATO vulnerability in Europe in the 1960s and 1970s.

It is important not to exaggerate the end of the Cold War in 1989–91 as a break, because many geopolitical issues spanned the divide, while much of the American and British capability deployed in the 1990s and 2000s stemmed from Cold War procurement policies, tasking and doctrine. The ability to fight a conventional war in Europe had to be translated to other spheres, which created problems in adaptation, and pressure for transformation; but much of the capability was already in place. In the case of Britain, however, the process of transformation to meet new goals was, especially in the initial stages, very much moulded by the drive to keep costs down. In part, this was a consequence of the serious economic and fiscal downturn of the early 1990s. *Options for Change*, the 1991 defence review, responded to the end of the Cold War by cutting all three services, and most radically the army: its strength was slashed from 156,000 men to 104,000. This 'peace dividend' was cost driven, rather than reflecting any clear sense of likely burdens. In particular, there was a lack of understanding of possible future threats; specifically, the requirements for peacekeeping and the problem of retaining a capacity for high-intensity warfare were underestimated. Indeed, the situation was even worse than this, because *Options for Change* was presented *after* the Gulf War had revealed serious deficiencies in the ability of the military, and particularly the army, to mount a major operation far from its bases without having to scavenge for the required resources. In the event, force projection was to be a feature of British military policy from 1990.

Options for Change was indeed a poorly conducted exercise. Work on a 'peace dividend' had started in 1990, after the collapse of Communism, but it was not completed before the Gulf War began. In August 1990, the projected cut in the army was of about one sixth, to a force of 126,000. That seemed reasonable, given the interest in out-of-area operations, which had just been given fresh impetus by Britain's help with the Namibian elections. More UN operations were anticipated: with the exception of Cyprus, Britain had not played a part in these since the Korean War. Cyprus was also an aberration as far as UN operations were concerned because, instead of relying on the UN logistic chain, the British forces had been supplied from the Sovereign Base in Cyprus, producing false lessons for the future.

However, by December 1990, the figure for the army had been reduced to 104,000 by the small group of civil servants assembled by Defence Secretary Tom King to process *Options*. It is unclear how they arrived at that number, which was not much larger than the RAF, which they left at 85,000 to man just under 600 combat aircraft. The Swedes manned virtually the same number of aircraft with 7,500 people, 5,000 of whom were conscripts, and there was no explanation of why almost 80,000 more servicemen than that were required to man the RAF.

John Major, who knew nothing about the armed forces and admitted to being scared stiff of how to speak to them when he paid his first visit to the Gulf, returned entranced. After visiting them again, after the end of the Gulf War, he came back and said that no action on *Options for Change* would be taken until the lessons of the war had been absorbed. In the war, the all-teeth army units used had been found to be too small, and so had had to be reinforced by at least a sub-unit drawn from elsewhere. Furthermore, the support branches proved quite incapable of supporting the force: Britain had to borrow ambulances from countries such as Canada and Romania; ad hoc transport and repair units were thrown together under ad hoc command arrangements; and equipment specialists had to be flown out to the Gulf because their army counterparts had been axed in earlier cuts.

The British force structure had been designed around the requirement to maintain 55,000 troops in Germany in order to man the allotted 65 kilometres of Inner German Border. In short, manpower sums had been threat based, a situation exacerbated by the position in Northern Ireland. Now, however, there was no guide as to the contingencies that had to be planned for; only an inevitable demand for money to be cut from the defence budget.

Rather than taking the time to absorb the lessons from the Gulf War, Major gave in to King's pressure to give MPs the details of *Options for Change* before the summer recess. This forced the army to decide in only six weeks how to cut its strength from 156,000 to 104,000 men while maintaining a balanced force. The cut was excessive, and the fact that the RAF is now down to half its 1991 numbers indicates the extent to which the distribution of cuts in *Options for Change* was poorly conceived.

Had the Major government done its sums properly, it would have realized that there was a need for an army of about 125,000 men, so that Britain, if it chose, could play its part in interventionist operations, which would inevitably be manpower intensive. Instead, equipment options should have been examined, particularly the Eurofighter, which was designed for a task that was no longer relevant – to keep Soviet aircraft at arm's length over the North Sea – and totally destabilized the defence budget. The Eurofighter completely failed the second of Field Marshal Lord Carver's affordability tests: can you afford it or can you afford to give up what you have to give up in order to be able to afford it?

Separate from the issue of appropriate force projection, the apparent legitimacy of such interventionism was (and still is) a different matter, not only because of the contentious nature of particular episodes, but also because, particularly from 2001, interventionism has been especially identified with the particular ideologies of the American administration of the period. This indicates the central role of 'tasking', the goals set by political direction, and also the plasticity or changeability of what is referred to as strategic culture, a term that can suggest a misleading degree of consistency. This was highlighted by discussion in 2004 as to how far the result of the highly contested presidential election would affect American foreign policy and what the consequences would be for Britain.

The extent to which American developments in force projection have not been matched at anywhere near the same level by other powers is an important aspect of world politics. The state that benefited most in economic terms from the 1990s, China, has – so far at least – concentrated rather on enhancing its short-range projection capability, thus mirroring the military consequences of Japan's economic growth of the 1970s and 1980s. Indeed, the contrast between the force structures and doctrines of China and those of Britain and France indicates the role of politics in shaping military capability and tasks as strategic cultures.

More significantly, American developments have not been matched elsewhere by advances in anti-strategy, operational practice, tactics or weaponry – i.e. in responses to the strategy, etc. of the leading power. (Hitherto, the general pattern in military history *on land* has been to have any advances in capability matched by other powers.) Saddam Hussein, for example, appears instead to have anticipated that the problems of urban warfare would reduce the American technological advantage and lead to casualties that would oblige the American government to change policy. (This analysis was certainly mistaken in the short term, and anyway could not prevent conquest by a well-organized and high-tempo American-dominated invasion force. Similarly, his hopes that international pressure or obstruction would prevent the Americans from acting proved an inaccurate reading of the dynamics of contemporary international relations.)

That American advances in military capability were not matched (at least in the sense of being effectively countered) does not establish a general rule that they cannot be, and it has indeed been suggested that the wide dissemination of new technologies, such as cruise-missile design and production, poses problems for the Americans. The issue highlights the degree to which one of the real problems of both military history and military analysis is deciding how best to analyse and generalize from examples. This is linked to an issue that divides analysts, namely whether and how far recent and current changes in capability constitute a military revolution, or a paradigm shift in military capability and warmaking; and, if they do, what results – and what consequences – this might have in terms both of analysing long-term trends in military capability, and of considering norms of behaviour within the international system.

The claims made for such a shift by military supporters, both in post and retired, both individual civilian commentators and military-industrial companies, are bold; yet they also offer instructive clues as to their limitations. For example, Northrop Grumman's 2004 advertisements for its ability to define the future ISTAR battle space (under the slogan 'Share information. Share victory') focused on the aerial vehicles and warships it linked in a blue world of sea and sky that left no room for the complexities of control on land.

If there is a military revolution to match the greatly enhanced and partly redirected investment seen in American 'defence' budgets, and at least the redirected profile of the British forces, then this does indeed raise the question of how far practices and theories of international relations will respond, or will need to respond. At the same time, the very same issues are posed by other attempted revolutions in military affairs, in particular those sought by terrorist groups and so-called rogue states. In the first case, the 2001 attempt by

Al-Qa'ida to use terrorist methods to strategic ends – by crippling, or at least symbolically dethroning, American financial and political power – failed, not least because it rested on a greatly flawed assumption about the concentrated and top-down nature of American power; but it also indicated the extent to which the terrorist repertoire was far from fixed. Although it is true that Al-Qa'ida did not deploy weapons of mass destruction in 2001, its ability to make use of Western technology (in this case civilian aircraft), like its determination to ignore any boundaries between military and civilian, highlighted the military, as well as the political, challenge that is posed. Similarly, in 2004, a dependence on public transport was exploited in the terrorist attacks on Madrid. This terrorism is arguably a more serious issue for international relations than any problem posed by particular states, because, although terrorist groups are also involved in a competition for legitimacy, the very nature of a stateless entity means that it is not bound by the constraints that generally arise from claims to sovereign power. The military dimension is provided clearly by the extent to which the terrorist enemy is not necessarily dependent on a territorial space that can be attacked or occupied.

As a result, however plausible it is to argue that there are terrorist states, nevertheless the challenge posed by terrorist movements is apparently greater, especially as they can seek to base themselves in 'failed states', where it is difficult to take action against them, short of full-scale military intervention. Terrorism is part of a continuum of criminal warfare and is characterized by opportunistic attacks, and this makes it very difficult to counter or contain through deterrence. Although most terrorism is, in fact, aimed at states in the Third World, the challenge it poses is particularly significant for strong powers – especially the USA as the strongest, but also Britain. They have far less real need to fear attack by other states than do weaker countries; even if a country was able to attack the USA, its forces would very probably be defeated, and its territory could certainly be attacked in turn.

This distinction between states, however, is challenged by

the attempt on the part of so-called rogue states to acquire weapons of mass destruction and, equally seriously, the related delivery systems. Although the regular forces of states such as North Korea and Iran probably lack the capability and the ability in defence to defeat the conventional forces of stronger powers (which, in this case, means the USA), and certainly could not wage an effective offensive war, such weapons would enable them to threaten these forces and, perhaps even eventually, their home territory. The possession of such weapons by rogue states would also challenge the aspect of international aspirations and force projection represented by alliance systems.

If these are the key elements in the situation at present, this situation does not, in fact, encompass the large majority of states in the world: most are neither leading military powers nor 'rogue states', and are unlikely to play a prominent role so far as Britain is concerned. Much of the conceptual problem with military analysis, as indeed with military history, stems from the extent to which it focuses on leading powers, with the corresponding assumption that other states seek to match, or at least to copy aspects of, their warmaking capacity and methods: the notion of paradigm powers. This approach assumes a unitary tasking (and analytical methodology) that is, in fact, inaccurate. For example, in many states, particularly but not exclusively in post-independence Latin America, sub-Saharan Africa and Oceania, the prime purpose of the military is internal control, and the army, in particular, is an arm of the state to this end. (In years to come, this may be the situation that faces the EU if it incorporates the Balkan states and Turkish Kurdistan.)

In territorial terms, the challenge in many states today comes not so much from foreign powers as from domestic regional opposition to the state – some of it separatist in character – or from resistance that has a social dimension, such as peasant risings. The resulting warfare, most of which assumes a guerrilla and/or terrorist character on the part of the rebels, is asymmetrical. It can also overlap considerably with struggles to combat crime, and specifically with wars on drugs. Thus, in

Mexico in the early 2000s, the army was used against the powerful drugs gangs, while a paramilitary Federal Investigations Agency was established to the same end. In functional terms, this might seem to have little to do with war as conventionally defined, but the firepower used by both sides was considerable. In Colombia, the left-wing FARC and the right-wing AUC paramilitaries are both involved in drugs. The British navy plays an important role in drug interception in the Caribbean; valuable in itself, this role is also significant in British relations with Caribbean allies, and is emphasized in recruitment for the navy.

The porous and contested definition of war suggested by its current usage – as in 'war on drugs' or 'war on terror', let alone 'war on poverty' – further complicates understanding of force and legitimacy, and makes it difficult to define the military. If the 'war on terror' is crucial, then the Saudi security forces that carry out armed raids against Al-Qa'ida suspects in which people are killed are as much part of the military as are conventional armed forces. Indeed, paramilitaries play an important role in many states, not least in internal control. Similarly, troops are employed for policing duties, as in Quetta in Pakistan in March 2004, when they restored order after a terrorist attack on a Shi'a procession had sparked a riot.

The challenge to states from domestic opposition is 'internationalized', in so far as there may be foreign support for such opposition, or, increasingly from the 1990s, international humanitarian concern over the issue. On the whole, however, the nature of conflict within states reflects an important aspect of international relations, namely the extent to which the use of force within sovereign areas is generally accepted. This practice is seen as a challenge to humanitarian interventionist precepts, but the latter usually lack military support unless they conform to the goals of great-power diplomacy.

The extent to which the conflation of humanitarianism with such goals sets a challenge to modern Western militaries has been apparent since the early 1990s, and was a particular issue in Kosovo in 1999. This challenge raises difficult issues of effectiveness, as Rwanda displayed and Darfur threatened to do, while the legitimacy of force is also an important question. The issue is also likely to become more of a topic in doctrine, though probably not to the same extent in weapons procurement, apart from accentuating the need for airlift capability.

If the state therefore emerges as a crucial intersection between force and international relations, this is scarcely new, but serves as a reminder that the state and its military capability can be seen to be acting in different ways and on several levels. The challenge for international relations theory is to address this variety. Current speculation about the relationship between force and international relations needs to address the future, not least because concepts of legitimacy and practices of legitimation in part depend on the likelihood of future consent. The pace of technological change is also a factor. New weapons systems create problems for judgement that reflect competing norms in international relations. Take the case of SDI/Star Wars: its advocates stress its defensive nature, but its critics include those who resist the idea of militarizing space.

In the early 2000s, again reflecting disagreements over norms and goals, the key issues in international relations were variously presented as a response to rogue states and terrorism, or to unilateral American (from a British perspective, Anglo-American) pro-active interventionism. It is likely that these will continue to be key issues, but it is improbable that they will continue to so dominate the agenda as they did in the early 2000s. In some respects, even then this agenda was misleading, as there were other conflicts and confrontations that were of great importance, and not just for humanitarian reasons: the war in Congo or the serious rivalry between India and Pakistan. The apparently dominant agenda of the early 2000s reflected American interests, perceptions and commitments, and the response of others to the USA – an important aspect of the extent to which the Western perception of developments (as of military history) can crowd out other changes worthy of attention.

It is unclear whether this perception will remain valid in future decades, as China becomes a more prominent power, and also because the majority of conflicts in the world do not involve Western powers, and it is uncertain how far the West will feel it necessary to intervene. This, indeed, has always been a consideration, apart from during the brief heyday of Western imperialism. China is often mentioned by theorists as likely to become involved in some future confrontation with the USA, largely on the 'neo-realist' assumption that states naturally expand and compete when they can, and that China's ambitions will lead it to clash with the USA. This, however, is less plausible than a regional ambition on the part of China that would involve India, Japan and Russia more closely than the USA. Indeed, the USA would have a choice over how far to intervene. This serves as a reminder that the world international system involves a number of complex regional situations, with the USA taking the leading role not because it is able to dominate the other powers (as might be implied by the word 'hegemony'), but rather because, aside from its largely uncontested regional dominance of the Americas and the Pacific, it is the sole state able to play a part in these other regional situations.

At this point, history and the future combine to underline the problem of conceiving of the relationship between force and legitimacy in Western terms – allowing, of course, for the great variety in the latter. Such a conception can be seen as central to modern discussion, as the theories and analytical terms employed are those of Western intellectual culture and legal analysis, but this can provide only limited guidance as to the response of others.

Whatever the extent of the military revolution, any conflict with the Soviet Union in Germany would have been very difficult for the Americans and their allies, including the British. It would have demonstrated the problems presented by the so-called direct approach, namely engaging the leading opposing force head on. The conflict would also have gone nuclear either from the outset or very rapidly. Instead, the Americans and British were to fight a ground war on very different terrain, and against a very different opponent: Iraq. This war, waged in 1991, was the product of Anglo-American engagement in the area, but, like the Falklands War, it arose from an unexpected act of aggression.

In the meantime, the navy's traditional function of protecting trade had, in response to the outbreak of the Iran–Iraq War in 1980, led to the establishment of the Armilla patrol in the Persian Gulf. This continued until its responsibilities broadened in 1990 with the Iraqi attack on Kuwait. The patrol, like the Falklands War, revealed the continued importance of the fleet in tackling unexpected tasks. There was a clear response in terms of force structure, with the retention of carrier and amphibious capability and the ordering of new ships. The carrier *Invincible* was on the verge of being sold to Australia in early 1982 when the Falklands War broke out. It was retained. Although *Bulwark* was broken up in 1984 and *Hermes* sold to India in 1986, the carrier *Illustrious*, built in 1976–82, entered service, as did a new *Ark Royal* built in 1978–85. Seventeen frigates were laid down in 1982–91. However, the major commitment was to the nuclear deterrent. Four 16,000-ton Vanguard-class submarines, armed with Trident missiles, the replacement to Polaris, were laid down in 1986–93 and the first, *Vanguard*, was commissioned in 1993.

By then, the strategic landscape had changed. The need to face new tasks was driven home by the Iraqi invasion of oil-rich Kuwait on 2 August 1990. The response defined high-spectrum warfare for the following decade, and for the British was the first major conflict fought against the conventional forces of another state since the Falklands War. The Americans took very much the leading role, but the British made a valuable contribution at sea, in the air and on land. Iraq's refusal to meet a UN deadline for withdrawal led, on 17 January 1991, to the start of a major air offensive, in which the British played a prominent role. This offensive worked because of the rapid success in overcoming the sophisticated Iraqi anti-aircraft system. Saddam Hussein had used French and Soviet technology to produce an integrated system, in which computers linked radars and missiles. The destruction of the air-defence system was a triumph not only for weaponry, but also for planning: it made full use of the opportunities presented by the weapons, but at the same time also out-thought the Iraqis, for example by getting them to bring their radars to full power, and thus exposing them to attack. As a result of the subsequent air assault, the Iraqi ground forces were short of supplies, their command and control system was heavily disrupted, so that they could not 'understand' the battle, and their morale was low.

In February 1991, Iraq was driven from Kuwait in a swift campaign in which the Iraqis were out-generalled and out-fought by coalition forces that benefited not only from superior technology, but also from their ability to maintain a high-tempo offensive while executing a well-conceived plan that combined air and land forces. Coalition fighting quality, unit cohesion, leadership and planning all played a major role in ensuring victory, as did Iraqi deficiencies in each. For the British, the war raised issues of force projection, logistics, and interoperability, although this last was eased by the experience of cooperation through NATO. The war was short, saw few British casualties, and did not divide the country. It did not lead to any occupation of Iraq and the ease of exit contrasted markedly with the Gulf War of 2003.

The next Western intervention in which the British played a role was not Somalia or Haiti, in both of which the Americans played a major role, but Yugoslavia. Western intervention to end the conflict there was undermined by a combination of US reluctance (not least from the military leadership) and European weakness, but settlements were eventually imposed in Bosnia in 1995, and in Kosovo in 1999, at the expense of the expansionism and ethnic aggression of a Serbian regime that unsuccessfully sought Russian sponsorship.

In 1998, the *Strategic Defence Review* outlined an expeditionary military strategy, and the following year a leading role was taken in the Kosovo crisis. The Major government had been reluctant to act over Bosnia, but its Blair successor played a much more active, and moralistic, role over Kosovo and then tried to take the credit for the success. In practice, the eventual Serb withdrawal may have owed more to a conviction, based in part on Russian information, that a NATO land attack was imminent and to the withdrawal of Russian support, than to the air offensive. However, French, German and, eventually, US rejection of British pressure for such an invasion indicated their doubts as to its feasibility. Indeed, a land attack faced a serious logistical challenge, and was dependent on the willingness of neighbouring countries to provide access and bases. In this case, Greek opposition to pressure on Serbia was a major hindrance. The Greek government had considerable sympathy for Serbia, largely due to a pan-Orthodox hostility to Muslims, but also partly to concern about revisionism and specifically its fear that an independent Kosovo would contribute to Macedonian expansionism at the expense of Greek control of areas that could be claimed by Macedonia.

George Robertson, the secretary of state for defence, publicly scorned commentators who warned about the difficulty of winning the Kosovo conflict by airpower alone, and also about the contrast between output (bomb and missile damage) and outcome. The subsequent Serbian withdrawal from Kosovo revealed, however, that NATO estimates of the damage inflicted by air attack, for example on Serb tanks, had been considerably exaggerated. Capitalizing on the limitations of Allied intelligence information and the serious consequences of this for Allied targeting, and benefiting from the serious impact of the weather on air operations (with a large number cancelled or otherwise affected), the Serbs employed simple and inexpensive camouflage techniques that took advantage of terrain and wooded cover and succeeded in preserving most of their equipment, despite 10,000 NATO strike sorties. Furthermore, the air offensive had not prevented the continuing large-scale expulsion of Kosovans from their homes, and this badly compromised the success of the operation. Indeed, Operation Horseshoe, the ethnic cleansing campaign, increased as the air attack intensified.

The difficulties facing any land attack contributed to the mistake of not preparing adequate options in the event of the air offensive failing. In the event, the crisis suggested that airpower would be most effective as part of a joint strategy, for ground and air threats to the Serbs were not separate. The eventual threat to the Serbs on the ground from a NATO invasion made their forces vulnerable to air attack, as it made dispersal, rather than concentration, a less viable proposition. Although the damage to the Serbian army from air attack was limited, the devastation wrought on Serbia's infrastructure, in the shape of bridges, factories and electrical power plants, was important, not least because it damaged the financial interests of the elite as well as their morale, and affected the functioning of the economy. Thus, there was a marked contrast between the tactical and strategic impact of airpower.

The Kosovo conflict revealed serious, although not unbridgeable, strains in NATO, as well as various limitations in advanced militaries. This included the British, although it is important to note that the Americans also encountered problems. Concerns about the effectiveness of their Apache helicopter in the Balkan terrain were particularly important, although, as an attack helicopter, the Apache offered both the Americans and the British shock action with its Hellfire missile, as well as an important surveillance capability. The report produced in 2000 by the National Audit Office on British operations the previous year revealed major problems with the RAF. On cloudy days, the planes were unable to identify targets and were grounded – something that, ironically, prevented an excessive depletion of bombs (the Americans suffered this with their cruise missiles). In addition, many bombs mounted on aircraft were unable to survive the shock of take-off, while heat and vibration damage affected missiles, and Tornado jets were reportedly unable to drop precision-guided bombs effectively. A lack of lift capacity led to a reliance on Russian-built Antonovs, hired from private contractors, but whose use was dependent on Russian certification. Furthermore, the SA80 rifle, the main British infantry weapon, was found to be faulty, and Serbian forces were readily able to monitor British radio communications.

NATO was also affected by uncertainty over tasking. Differences within the alliance hindered a clear articulation of mission and the stages of its achievement. This helped ensure an incremental plan of air attack that both failed to overcome Serbian resolve and contributed to a somewhat negative impression of airpower capability. There were also more profound strategic problems, not least those posed by the goal of stopping Milosević from pursuing a particular policy in Kosovo while not seeking his overthrow. The determination to detach Russia from Serbia, and not to defeat the latter to the point that the Kosovan separatists were able to win independence, complicated the situation and helped ensure that the hesitation that stemmed from NATO consensus building had a political rationale.

Milosević's determination to thwart NATO goals by stepping up ethnic cleansing enabled, or rather forced, NATO to overcome many of its differences on political and military strategy, and instead to act. This, however, also exposed the shortcomings of NATO planning. Only a very short air offensive had been anticipated, with relatively few aircraft involved. There was inadequate preparation for Serbian persistence, not least a failure in operational plans and in targeting systems. There was also a more general inability to work with the unpredictability of the situation, ranging from poor weather to the difficulties of assessing Serbian responses.

Furthermore, the length of the campaign created greater political pressure and more reasons for disagreement, and all within a context in which commanders and those doing the targeting were constrained by the strict parameters set by a determination to minimize civilian losses and to ensure no Allied losses – a goal that ruled out ground operations. Thus, strategically, operationally and tactically, the military had to plan in ways that compromised doctrinal 'purity'; these constraints were made acceptable by the inability of the Serbs to inflict serious damage on NATO forces, which ensured that the costs of President Clinton's aversion to risk, and the impact of NATO differences, were both contained. The operation tested NATO, but also resulted in a major extension of its mission, as it saw a large-scale intervention outside NATO's borders. Nevertheless, Kosovo did not lead to casualties or difficulties sufficient to sap domestic support, and the same was true of the manageable intervention in Sierra Leone in 2000. A level of stability was established in Kosovo.

The Kosovo conflict is generally seen in terms of the Allied air assault, with the addition of the prospect of a land invasion. There was also, however, a naval dimension that reflected the reconfiguration of naval power and that was the product of both opportunity and need. The *Options for Change* defence review of 1991 had outlined a cut in naval personnel of 3,000, while the submarine fleet was to be reduced from 27 to 16. Under its 1994 sequel, *Frontline First*, naval personnel were to be cut by a further 1,900. This was the smallest reduction in the review, but the navy contained fewer personnel than the army or the air force. In response to these cuts and the need to find a post-Cold War mission, the navy developed a doctrine of amphibious assault and power projection into the littoral, using helicopter-borne forces and cruise missiles. As a result, targets and goals were land based. This echoed the strategy underlining the investment in Polaris and Trident, but linked it to the surface fleet, although submarines did remain important. In 1998, the submarine *Splendid* achieved Britain's first live firing of a Tomahawk cruise missile, a weapon bought from the USA. The following year, *Splendid* fired these missiles at Serb targets in Kosovo as part of the NATO operations there. In Operation Allied Force, sorties were also launched from *Invincible*. The 22,000-ton helicopter carrier *Ocean*, completed in 1998 as a commando carrier for the marines, and the assault ship *Fearless* were also deployed to provide the capability for a marine assault, although, in the event, none was launched.

Earlier, in support of the pressure on Iraq, *Invincible* had been deployed to the Persian Gulf on three missions in 1996–9. Similarly, the RAF was responsible for enforcing No Fly Zones in Iraq. Naval power projection continued into the early 2000s. In October 2001, cruise missiles fired from *Trafalgar* and *Triumph* were used in the initial bombardment of Afghanistan. In the winter of 2002–3, British warships played a major part in Operation Reinstate, the Anglo-American attempt to stop Iraqi oil smuggling. In 2003, British warships also provided an important supporting role in the attack on Iraq.

The 1998 *Strategic Defence Review* did not see homeland security as a real issue and made its dispositions accordingly, as is shown by its attitude to the Army Reserve. Events suggested that it had been overly optimistic. Blair captured the national mood in 2001 when he declared, on the evening of 11 September, that we in Britain would stand 'shoulder to shoulder' with our friends in the United States against the 'evil of mass terrorism'. The crisis stemming from the terrorist attacks on New York and Washington on 11 September 2001 led not to an emphasis on homeland security, but instead to a major extension of British military effort, a policy outlined in the 2002 *New Chapter*. This was more explicitly expeditionary in intention than the 1998 *Strategic Defence Review*, which envisaged the ability to support two concurrent small and medium-scale operations. Part of the extension of effort was within NATO and part was outside it. In response to the attacks, the USA sought help under Article Five of the North Atlantic Treaty, an article that committed the allies to regarding an attack on one as an attack on all, and this was agreed on 12 September. In specific terms, the lack of a state against which to mount an immediate response ensured that the particular assistance requested was modest. The USA asked NATO to send seven AWACS early-warning aircraft to help patrol American air space.

The USA moved swiftly on to the attack, first in Afghanistan in 2001 and then against Iraq in 2003. Britain played a secondary role in Iraq, but still an important one because of the potential for overstretch created by the relatively small size of the force deployed by the Americans. The 125,000 US combat troops on the ground were the key element, compared to 45,000 troops from Britain and 2,000 from Australia. The value of the British and Australians was enhanced, however, because the campaign did not see the full commitment of forces originally envisaged: the Turks' refusal to allow an invasion across their frontier with Iraq ensured that troops from the American 4th Infantry Division, prepared for that invasion, could not be used at the outset of the war. The British played a key role in the south, but were too heavily committed there to offer effective assistance further north. Securing the oil infrastructure rapidly was a crucial objective in order to prevent a repetition of the destruction wrought by the Iraqis in Kuwait in 1991. Beginning on 20 March 2003, a night helicopter commando assault on the Al Faw peninsula was the first conventional-force ground action of the war, and the first British opposed helicopter assault since Suez in 1956. Naval, air and ground fire supported the operation. The rapid advance of the 7th Armoured Brigade to the west indicated the range of capability.

The British ability to act in 2003 was greater than during the first Gulf War thanks to the lessons learned: preparations had been made for a rerun of the war, and appropriate deployments had been made in the meantime. This applied both to operations to deter Iraq, such as the enforcement of the No Fly Zones, and to deployments elsewhere in the region. Exercise Saif Sareea (Swift Sword) in Oman in 2001 was particularly important in building up operational experience in specific difficult conditions. This was also true of the deployment of troops in Afghanistan. As a result of this background, it became easier to act rapidly in the region.

The response cycle was not limited to operating in the Persian Gulf. There was also a response to the successive operations elsewhere that Britain engaged in. For example, the Kosovo campaign indicated the deficiencies of air warfare, in part because the accuracy of the bombs was limited. In response, the laser-guided bombs were made more accurate by adding Global Positioning System (GPS) guidance with an inertial back-up, an enhancement introduced into the operational system in April 2002. The GPS coordinates could be programmed in the planes while they were airborne, providing enhanced flexibility in time-sensitive targeting. Greater accuracy ensured that the weight of the bombs required could be reduced.

Other weapons were also successfully introduced. Storm Shadow was used in 2003 – a weapon that had a considerable stand-off range and a high degree of accuracy, aided by en route navigation systems, and that was able to penetrate reinforced concrete. The stand-off range reduced vulnerability to ground fire and air interception. The RAF's enhanced capability was not simply a matter of bombing and associated air support. There was also an increase in air-to-air effectiveness, although it did not come into play in 2003 because the Iraqi air force did not contest control of the air. The role of the Tornado F3 was enhanced by improvements in radar, radio links, and armament in the shape of ASRAAM, the Advanced Short Range Air-to-Air Missile. There was a similar improvement in American capability, and the net effect was an air superiority during the conflict that provided the opportunity for bombing and air support that was only contested from the ground. That, however, remains an important challenge to air attack.

On the whole, the war demonstrated the advantages brought by new weaponry information systems, but also the continued friction of the battlefield and the problems involved in coalition operations – even between the USA and Britain, with their long experience of joint training. Interoperability is of crucial importance in avoiding fratricide.

Key army weaponry, particularly the Challenger 2 tank, the Warrior infantry fighting vehicle, and the AS 90 self-propelled artillery, all worked well. Nevertheless, the campaign also revealed problems with providing equipment when required, most conspicuously upgraded flak jackets. In part, this was a matter of the difficulties of a fast-moving campaign. However, there was also the more serious question of a contrast between cost-consciousness, with its emphasis on 'just sufficient' provision, and the friction and uncertainty that lead to the more costly 'just-in-case' scenario. The Defence Select Committee's report on operations in Iraq indicated the need for significant improvements.

More generally, in the 1990s and early 2000s, the individual services saw major changes in response to the shifts in goals, with the resulting emphasis on an expeditionary profile. This was crucial to the restructuring of the army, but also more generally. Naval capability was seen in joint terms because of an emphasis on cooperation with land and air forces. The Permanent Joint Headquarters for the conduct of joint operations, an objective very much pushed by the 1994 White Paper, was established in 1996, the year that saw the publication of a joint *British Defence Doctrine*. In 1997, the Joint Services Command and Staff College was set up, to be followed, after the 1998 *Strategic Defence Review*, by the Joint Doctrine and Concepts Centre. In July 2001, this Centre published a *Joint Vision* for the UK armed forces. The impact of this was also seen in the decision that the 1999 second edition of *British Marine Doctrine* would be the last written under the auspices of the Naval Staff, as all future editions would be written and published by the new Centre. This edition indeed declared:

> The maritime environment is inherently *joint*...Naval forces themselves exist to influence events ashore; they have never operated strategically in an exclusively naval environment...the sea is a pre-eminent medium because, above all, it provides access at a time and place of political choice. By history, tradition and skill the UK is better placed, certainly than any other European nation, to exploit this medium and to develop a strategic doctrine of warfare based on the joint use of the sea...Ultimately, maritime forces can only realise their considerable potential when integrated fully into a joint force.

Future Navy, the Navy Board's strategic vision, focuses on littoral warfare and power projection and regards joint requirements and capabilities as crucial.

The navy that was called upon to act was itself changing in force structure. In 1998, the *Strategic Defence Review* outlined cuts in warship and submarine numbers, although it did include a provision for the construction of two super-carriers, capable of acting as platforms for aircraft in a way that the anti-submarine carriers they were designed to replace had not been able to. This ran the risk of investing in an outdated force structure, as carriers provide readily identifiable targets for missiles, and their protection in wartime would require the use of other warships. It is unclear that the new carriers offer a marked advantage over comparable expenditure on the smaller Invincible-type carriers, which have repeatedly proved their versatility. It might have been better to invest in more of this type, which focus on helicopter and VSTOL aircraft and on supporting amphibious assault craft, rather than in fewer of the big carriers.

At the same time, the plan for a new generation of warships, centring as it did on carriers capable of operating around the world, was a reminder of the ongoing close relationship between British power and naval strength. This strength was presented as justifying Britain's continued claims to great-power status, for example her permanent seat on the United Nations Security Council. The carriers were designed for multiple roles: fighting naval battles, launching ground strikes and mounting amphibious missions. In 2003, Britain joined with France, Italy and Spain in agreeing to collaborate over maintaining the readiness of their aircraft carriers in order to ensure that one was on station at all times.

Britain was better placed than other European states to deploy naval power. When the agreement was reached in 2003, Britain had three carriers, and France, Italy and Spain one each. Naval power was enhanced from 1990 by the acquisition of *Ocean*, the largest warship in the fleet, as well as 16 Duke-class frigates and two 32,300-ton fleet replenishment ships, each able to carry five helicopters and, if necessary, Sea Harriers. The *Strategic Defence Review* also led to an increase in logistical capability, with the RAF having four C-17 Globemaster aircraft and the Royal Fleet Auxiliary using six RO-RO ships. This gave force to the 2003 Defence White Paper, which had argued that 'Priority must be given to meeting a wider range of expeditionary tasks, at greater range from the United Kingdom and with ever-increasing strategic, operational and tactical tempo.'

Critics focused on the decline in overall warship numbers, although the reduction was less pronounced than in the tank force, which lacked the mobility required for force projection.

On 5 June 2000, Iain Duncan Smith, the shadow defence secretary, complained in the House of Commons that the number of frigates and destroyers had fallen from 35 in 1997 to 27, and submarines from 15 to 10, while Gordon Prentice, a Labour MP, reported that 'we are flogging off at a knock-down price ships that are perfectly serviceable, that were only commissioned maybe 12 or 13 years ago'. In reply, John Spellar, the armed forces minister, noted that the *Strategic Defence Review* had shown that the requirement for major surface vessels had altered. In December 2003, the White Paper *Delivering Security in a Changing World* made provisions for fresh changes: 'Some of our older vessels contribute less well to the pattern of operations that we envisage, and reductions in numbers will be necessary.' As a result, in January 2004, it was decided to mothball four destroyers, not previously due to be decommissioned until 2007–10. This would reduce the number of escort ships to 28, compared with 32 French counterparts. The destroyers to be mothballed had, with their Sea Dart missiles, an important air-defence capability, but this no longer appeared so necessary.

The sense of betrayed heritage was palpable in the editorial of the *Daily Telegraph* on 6 January 2004, which began 'What would Nelson have said?' It was argued that Britain would no longer be able to mount major naval operations unless alongside the USA or France. Similar comments were made by journalists about plans to merge regiments, or when contrasting the number of planes with those at the time of the Battle of Britain. A sense of loss and foreboding characterized much of the public discussion, and served as a counterpoint to the instinctive anti-war approach taken by the other side. In practice, neither of these automatic responses had much to offer in terms of policy discussion or analysis. In the event, the 2004 defence review's projected cuts included three destroyers, three frigates, three submarines, four infantry battalions, and four aircraft squadrons, but there is also a programme of major naval expansion, including two aircraft carriers, six D class, Type 45 destroyers (the first of which, *Daring*, was launched on 1 February 2006), three large amphibious ships and a new class of submarine. The 2003 White Paper wanted the ability to support three concurrent small and medium-scale operations, and, to that end, stated the requirement to 'maintain a broad spectrum of maritime, land, air, logistics, C4ISR[2] and Special Forces capability elements to conduct limited national operations, or to be the lead or framework nation for coalition operations, at small to medium scale'. When matters reached the large scale, it was assumed, the USA would be involved and, as a result, it would be necessary to be able to operate with the US command and control structures.

While attention was focused on Iraq, there was a major extension in NATO's operational commitments. The 1999 Kosovo KFOR operation had been very much in Europe, even though outside the actual NATO area. But that was not the case with the commitment in Afghanistan, where, by 2005, NATO had, albeit with some difficulty, deployed tens of thousands of troops. Indeed, in the summer of 2003, NATO took command of ISAF, the International Security Assistance Force – a clear sign of an expeditionary capacity. This led to a focus on NRF, the NATO Response Force, which was inaugurated on 15 October 2003, conducting an initial demonstration exercise in Turkey the following month. The NRF was a capability not related to NATO's earlier established role of territorial defence. However much it was presented in terms of a reinterpretation of NATO's Strategic Concept, and however strongly it was endorsed by the Prague NATO Summit of November 2002 and the commitments made there to invest in the military, it lacked any real core of public support. This is what lay behind the difficulties in reaching political decisions for NATO action and in providing sufficient resources. It proved hard to generate forces for ISAF or, indeed, to obtain practical backing for the NRF from many NATO members, however much it was proclaimed a success. In part, this was a matter of cost, but there was a more general lack of political will, manifested in the serious national restrictions on the use of forces, which served to undermine operational responsiveness and effectiveness, and indeed morale.

Nevertheless, Jaap de Hoop Scheffer, who became NATO

secretary general in 2004, has pushed ahead with bold objectives, including making a major contribution to security in the Middle East and Central Asia, and taking a role in shaping the international security environment. Thus, the enhancement of military capabilities has been linked to a pro-active political mission. This is in line with the North Atlantic Treaty of 1949 on which NATO is based, but over a far greater range. Indeed, NATO commitments carefully excluded the imperial interests of member countries, such as the French in Algeria, let alone the Portuguese in Goa.

The general situation raises questions about the value of the NATO or EU envelope for British action, and that is underlined by difficulties in the division of labour within these organizations. There is much cooperation, but there are also important difficulties, and the process of transformation reflects a military objective that lacks comparable political action (as opposed to rhetoric). Burden sharing is a major issue, and this is made worse by falling defence budgets. About half the members of NATO are spending less than two per cent of GDP on defence, and this is becoming an increasingly common situation. The problem of a mismatch between public goals and budgets is one that politically adroit commanders skirt around, but it weakens the validity of alliance solutions to defence issues, whether the envelope is NATO or the EU. In December 2003, the latter produced a prospectus, *A Secure Europe in a Better World*, which pressed for an active response to threats posed by rogue or failed states, terrorism, regional conflicts, and weapons proliferation. In 1996, NATO foreign ministers had agreed to create a European Security and Defence Identity and to make NATO forces available to this end. Furthermore, the problem of inadequate expenditure is compounded by the way in which what is available is spent: much goes on established systems and on duplicated facilities, rather than on transformational capabilities. Moreover, the nature of procurement is sclerotic, while logistical support systems are inadequate at the supranational level and weak at the national level.

British power projection has also been encouraged by the

winding-down of the Northern Ireland commitment. In 1998, the year of the Good Friday Agreement, the last soldier was killed, ending a period from 1969 (when troops were deployed) in which 452 British military died there. Although the peace dividend proved slow to materialize, by 2005, and after much prevarication, there were positive moves toward IRA disarmament, although fresh concerns were raised in early 2006. Direct rule had been reimposed in 2002, but without a resumption of civil war. The relocation of British troops elsewhere led to a reduction of the army in Northern Ireland by 4,000 men. It is difficult to be confident, let alone sure, of IRA politics or goals, but the move toward peace in Northern Ireland certainly helped the government to focus on the Middle East.

At the same time, this focus exposed and encouraged serious problems in NATO and EU unity. This was not only a matter of the opposition shown by France, Germany and Belgium to Anglo-American policy in the run-up to the Iraq War, but also subsequently. A clear example was provided by the Spanish election of March 2004. Although the victorious Socialist Party leader, Jose Luis Zapatero, subsequently stated that opposing terrorism would be his top priority, his unilateral decision to withdraw troops from Iraq appeared to indicate that Al-Qa'ida terrorism, in the shape of the Madrid bombings, could have an impact on policy – the very message that other powers were trying not to send. Furthermore, the withdrawal of troops led to an additional burden on other members of the coalition, including Britain. The same month as the Spanish election, the different responses of NATO's European members to NATO's request for more troops in Kosovo (Britain, Germany, France and Denmark said yes; others said no) again indicated that burden sharing within the alliance was not working. The extent to which, in the Iraq crisis, Britain compromised its ability to take independent initiatives by being so closely linked with the USA in the minds of others (interoperability in part being a matter of perception) is a matter for debate.

Europe, however, does not offer a comfortable alternative.

A Common Foreign and Security Policy was developed as the second 'pillar' of the Treaty of European Union signed by the European Union members at Maastricht in December 1991. Blair committed himself to this policy in 1998, and it led to the development of a European Defence and Security Policy focused on the creation of a 60,000-strong European Rapid Reaction Force. This proved overly ambitious, as did certain attempts at shared military provision (for example, in the 1990s, the Anglo-French-Italian Horizon project), but EU forces have been deployed in the Balkans and in Congo. However, aside from the EU's weaknesses in military capability and delivery, there are problems with decision making, with responsiveness being overly slow. National contributions do not mean command flexibility, and creating such flexibility may well lessen the willingness to provide contributions. Reform and politics make poor bedfellows in the EU.

1 Lawrence Freedman, *The Official History of the Falklands Campaign* (London, 2005), vol. I, p. 191.
2 The military functions of: Command, Control, Communications, Computer, plus Intelligence, Surveillance and Reconnaissance information.

CHAPTER 3

CURRENT PROBLEMS

> ...we no longer need to retain a capability against the re-emergence of a direct conventional strategic threat to the United Kingdom or our allies. Priority must be given to meeting a wider range of expeditionary tasks, at greater range from the United Kingdom and with ever-increasing strategic, operational, and tactical tempo.
>
> *Delivering Security in a Changing World*
> White Paper, December 2003

Defence policy unites several key problems facing Britain. It stands at the junction of foreign and fiscal policy, external goals and domestic security. Defence policy has to respond to rapidly changing circumstances; at the same time, an able execution of its unpredictable tasks requires adequate preparation in the shape of appropriate doctrine, training and weaponry. These problems are amply demonstrated at the present time, confronting as they do defence professionals, government and opposition politicians seeking to define policy, and external commentators. Indeed, the range of unpredictability has increased greatly over the past decade. In part this is due to the marked rise in power projection that has been a feature of New Labour's internationalism – a rise that was in no way inevitable and the merits of which can be queried on defence grounds.

There is scant sign of this rise abating, although the sources of the internationalism do vary greatly. There are two particular strands of activity: opposition to terrorism and humanitarianism, although the shape that each takes is very much the product of the interaction of circumstances with the responses of politicians. In addition, alongside power projection – and in its wake – comes the role of the military as an occupation force, holding the ring in the absence of peaceful civil government. Thus, the military has seen the Northern Ireland experience extrapolated, albeit in very different contexts. The difference of the contexts poses a particular problem because, while the military used to pride itself on its skill in counter-insurgency operations, it is unclear whether, despite the dedication and professionalism much in evidence, the legacy of Iraq and Afghanistan may not seriously challenge this impression. In turn, this may lead to questions about capability and doctrine. Skill in counter-insurgency has led to contrasts with American military doctrine and training and with associated political practices, and to the repeated suggestion that these undermined stabilization in Iraq. These criticisms of the Americans may indeed be justified, but it is less clear that the British approach will be any more successful.

Then there is the problem of a failed state at home, or rather of the inability of government to secure the rule of law. In 1984–5, large numbers of police were deployed in the East Midlands during the miners' strike, where they successfully employed the tactics of crowd control developed in Northern Ireland. Indeed, in what was a clear crisis in British democracy, with a revolutionary Marxist trade union leadership seeking to use industrial muscle to thwart the views of a democratically elected government in a key policy area, the government was able to rely on the police to achieve its goals and did not need to turn to the army. From the 1980s, the police gradually became less of a local force for crime prevention, more of it was armed, and sections received training from the military, although it would be going too far to claim that the police became paramilitary. The lack of central control and the absence of more than a limited armed capability ensured that such a description was inadequate. Nevertheless, the gulf between police and army has narrowed, with important implications for requirements from the latter.

In the early 2000s, in contrast to 1984–5, there was a more direct reliance on the army. In the face of the blockades of fuel depots in September 2000, the government considered using force to reopen supply routes. John Prescott, the deputy prime minister, declared that the government could not retreat in the face of the fuel protests, renegotiating taxes 'at a refinery gate, under threat of 60 days' notice', while Blair argued that 'No government can act on the basis of people threatening to bring the country to a halt.' In fact, shocked by the crisis and uncertain of the police, the government abandoned the policy of raising fuel duties by more than inflation, a concession that helped make a mockery of their energy and environmental policies. However, in late 2000, the government responded to the possibility of a resumption of the petrol depot blockades by training 1,000 soldiers to drive oil tankers so that picket lines could be breached. The following year, the military fulfilled a key command and control role during the serious outbreak of foot-and-mouth disease, offering a capability that looked toward future challenges in the shape of human pandemics. The military, indeed, have capabilities that the civil authorities lack. The Civil Contingencies Act of 2004 and the creation of the Civil Contingencies Secretariat in the Cabinet Office understandably emphasize the non-military dimension, but a capacity to provide military assistance is necessary for government.

The government's ability to turn to the army to provide coverage during the firemen's strike of 2002 was important in enabling it to resist the challenge to pay restraint. Indeed, at a time when the invasion of Iraq was being planned, this was an instructive guide to the range of tasks, and therefore capabilities, demanded of the military. This was taken further when terrorism became a key element in the threat to Britain. The deployment of troops, most obviously at Heathrow airport in February 2003, was a very public demonstration of concern about this threat. Troops from the Household Cavalry Regiment and the Grenadier Guards were sent to provide assistance to the police at a time when an intelligence report indicated an Al-Qa'ida plan to hijack a plane in Eastern Europe, where security is lower than in Britain, and then to fly it into a passenger terminal at Heathrow. Concern about such plans led also to instructions to the RAF to shoot down passenger jets that had been hijacked – a total change to earlier policy.

Terrorism was scarcely new, and the bombing of Pan Am 103 over Lockerbie in 1988 remains the single, biggest terrorist outrage on or over British soil. It was also an atrocity that demonstrated the extent to which the British homeland could be involved in wider struggles. Yet the pace of concern increased as a result of the real and reported activities of Al-Qa'ida, whose attacks in the USA on 11 September 2001 led to the death of 67 British citizens, an indication of the extent to which Britain is closely involved in the American economy, and, indeed, of the practical consequences of globalization: by then, about ten million British citizens lived and worked abroad.

The military are not in the frontline of counter-terrorism. That is the job of the security services and, in support of them, the police. Nevertheless, if necessary, the military is an important support. This indeed was not new. Back in 1950, the shooting down of a Soviet civil aircraft carrying an atomic bomb on a suicide mission was a hypothetical scenario considered by the government. Nevertheless, that was not the way the Soviet Union operated. Nor indeed was nuclear or biological or chemical terrorism an aspect of the IRA portfolio. The challenges these pose to the civil authorities are such that the military would be called on to help deal with the consequences if they occurred, but also suggest the need to take a pro-active stance in whatever form. In terms of the threat scenario, terrorism is currently greater than challenges from foreign states. It is unclear that this will last, but the ability of terrorism to help set the agenda (an ability greatly accentuated by media coverage) does act as a stimulus to action. Meanwhile, the nihilistic nature of terrorist assumptions tends to promote violence, as does the very limited prospect of terrorist causes making headway through democratic support, at least in mainland Britain. The nature of defence against such a threat is not one that can generally be expressed in military terms. Instead, there are more complex issues of security that include changes to the organizational methods of institutions, as well as a critical look at the 'spaces' created for terrorism by notions of civil liberties that have scant regard for the citizen's freedom from the threat of terrorism.

At the same time, the international pattern of terrorism is such that it is not helpful to separate home and foreign commitments and deployments; that said, the legal and operational contexts and constraints do vary greatly. Force projection to ensure security at home is a rationale of the Iraq War, particularly one voiced by George W. Bush. 'Draining the swamp' is a phrase commonly used. The contentious nature of this and other views on the war is such that analysis of the argument is far from easy. To a certain extent, this rationale risks the situation that occurs with all too many operations, namely fitting the operation to the existing capability and doctrine, rather than focusing on the task itself without such a fit (though that is never completely possible). At present, the notion of a range of terrorist challenges provides a role across current British force structure, with the prospect of 'rogue states' having and using weapons of mass destruction providing the high-spectrum component. This range, however, does not address the issue of priorities.

Providing everyone with a role is not the same as establishing priorities both in preparedness and in actual crises – a general problem with defence planning, particularly when it originates within a military reliant on a tri-service command structure and related doctrine. The problem of priorities arises in terms of the particular financial exigencies and political pressures Britain faces in specific conjunctures. And similar problems affect other states, including the most affluent, the USA. Phrased differently, strategic cultures are in an acute state of flux as a consequence not just of the pace of change across the world, but also of the impact, both internationally and domestically, of globalization and democratization. The latter poses an acute problem for military planning, as it leads to a pressure for openness that is incompatible with established practice. Indeed, any threat analysis becomes contentious, as the police have found over their typecasting of people for searching.

At present, the debate about military purpose and capability focuses on the consequences of the problems facing British policy, in particular in light of the difficulty of suppressing opposition in Iraq. In a reaction against the technology- and weapons-driven account of capability, there is an emphasis on the need to move from battle to war, and from engagement with regulars to struggle with irregulars. Having written in this vein, I can sympathize with this approach, but there is a danger of moving from one extreme to the other. Commentators who discuss the need for a doctrine and capability to deal with irregulars need to do so in order to prevent these factors from being ignored, rather than to deny any role for the alternative.

Indeed, there is a danger that present-mindedness will lead to a failure to grasp the range of current problems, let alone the nature of future ones. The USA has come to appreciate that problems in the Middle East should not lead to a neglect of the consequences of Chinese power, for example: this was recently driven home by news of Chinese arms purchases from Russia and by the development of the Shanghai Cooperation Organization, under the auspices of which a Russian–Chinese military exercise was held in August 2005. To a certain extent, the lesser global range of British power, combined with Blair's optimism about the possibility of solving other problems, has ensured that the British have not looked so far afield, and certainly not as far as East Asia. Indeed, the EU willingness to sell weaponry to China is understandably of great concern to the USA.

The British reluctance to engage with the strategic threat in East Asia is mistaken and is, to a certain extent, self-serving, although also understandable given the respective weight of British and American power. More generally, the threat challenges other aspects of British policy. For example, the Franco-German willingness to look to the Sino-Russian axis to balance the USA (and to take energy in large quantities from Russia) underlines the extent to which the Blair government's European policy is based on a strategic fallacy that may have serious long-term consequences. Any focus on the 'lessons' of Afghanistan and Iraq has to be put in a context that includes this strategic threat. The issue has a number of dimensions, not least force structure and doctrine.

The cost of an interventionist force profile is considerable, but far less than retaining cutting-edge readiness in all spheres.

However, due to the range of capabilities entailed by interventionist policies, these choices are not unrelated. At the present moment, and in the light of Blair's very public concern with humanitarian disasters in Africa, the range of options includes intervention in Sudan or Zimbabwe, which would certainly require air-attack and airlift capability. More generally, underlining the need for across-the-spectrum, cutting-edge readiness, the Gulf War showed that, before the counter-insurgency stage, there was first conventional conflict with the Iraqi regular military. There is no reason to believe that the same would not be true of other interventions, however much directed to humanitarian goals. Furthermore, whatever the goals of intervention, conflict or confrontation with other regular forces may arise. The ability to sustain convincingly a confrontation short of conflict is particularly valuable.

Confrontation redirects attention to the upper range of the military spectrum. This has become more acute because of nuclear proliferation, particularly by states not willing to comply with obligations under the Nuclear Non-Proliferation Treaty, most obviously Iran.

The third power to acquire atomic weaponry, Britain was committed by the late 1990s to a concept of minimum deterrent posture, with the weaponry serving as a leftover of the Cold War, when it provided a key role in deterrence as a guarantor of national security, and also as a guarantee against future risks. The 1998 *Strategic Defence Review* argued that 'in a changing and uncertain world, Britain continues to require a credible and effective nuclear deterrent based on the Trident submarine force'. This was reiterated in the *New Chapter* of 2002, the review of the *Strategic Defence Review*, and again in the Defence White Paper of 2003. This force also provides a symbol of military power, and one very much under political – rather than military – control. On 1 November 2005, John Reid, the defence secretary, told the Commons Defence Committee that 'it would be naïve to believe that there will be no further proliferation'. This made it unlikely that the process of nuclear disarmament that had accompanied, and been greatly accelerated by, the end of the Cold War would be extended, and thus obliged the government to consider how best to maintain the nuclear deterrent. Reid argued, correctly, that although nuclear weapons were no deterrent against terrorism, this did not mean that they were unnecessary. Instead, he emphasized the need to look decades ahead when considering threats. Britain has four Vanguard-class ballistic, nuclear submarines, each of which carries 16 Trident D-5 ballistic missiles, purchased, with their launch systems, from the USA. Each missile is capable of carrying twelve warheads that can engage different targets at once. However, the government is committed to sending each submarine out with only 48 warheads. The submarines are supported by a shore infrastructure. In turn, the capability requires investment in research and development. In July 2005, the Ministry of Defence announced that it was to spend £350 million over three years on upgrading facilities at the Atomic Weapons Establishment at Aldermaston.

Were Britain to fail to maintain its nuclear capability, it is likely that the USA would see Britain as a less potent ally, while France and Russia would be the sole European states with nuclear military power. These scenarios pose significant political risks, not least to a sense of power, that have to be set against the costs of replacing the Vanguard-class submarines (the first of which, assuming a five-year extension of service, needs replacing in about 2023), particularly the nuclear steam-raising plant and the warheads, and the danger that these costs will unbalance military expenditure and bring undesirable cuts elsewhere. As a result, the Ministry of Defence does not wish to bear the burden of the expenditure alone, and instead argues that, because the deterrent also serves political goals, money should come from the wider government budget. At present, the cost of the deterrent is modest – less than three per cent of the defence budget – largely because there is no procurement element and only modest manpower requirements. The acquisition costs of any replacement with a completely new system would be heavy, for consideration would have to be given not only to replacing the warheads, but also to the non-financial costs of using a different non-submarine-launched system. Choosing a land or air-based (most obviously cruise missile) delivery system would involve not only the problems of providing facilities in the face of public opposition, and of Britain becoming a target, but also of meeting the obligations under the Comprehensive Test Ban Treaty to eschew testing. As a result, the validity of a new warhead would be uncertain, which might well undermine its value as a deterrent. In contrast, a replacement warhead that relies essentially on the existing system could, under the terms of the Treaty, be tested in the laboratory at Aldermaston. Retaining a submarine-based capability maintains the flexibility, mobility, speed of delivery and stealth of the current system, and also enables the retention of the existing infrastructure. These points do not answer concerns about the usefulness or value of the deterrent as a whole, not least its value in response to asymmetric threats, but they help explain how best to retain a national nuclear capability that is affordable and workable.

The Iraq conflict has encouraged a sense that any major confrontation or conflict will take place in alliance with the USA, and the extent to which the Americans took part, eventually, in the Bosnia and Kosovo crises underlined this conviction. Such a conviction encourages an emphasis on interoperability with the American military, which is a major factor behind investment in high-spectrum military capability. This is a process encouraged by American leaders and commentators, who are keen to see Britain able to share in American force projection; but the net effect may well be to distort British procurement, force profile and doctrine. Furthermore, although the alignment with the USA is very valuable for Britain, these crises served to flag up the extent to which Britain could not set the terms of the intervention. If anything, the Iraq crisis has made the terms of future cooperation more difficult. This is true not so much of military, but of political factors. While trying to strengthen the Anglo-American alliance, Blair ironically has greatly damaged it, not only in terms of the particular issue of cooperation over Iraq, but also with reference to the general problem of the need in alliances for a confidence that cannot, in practice, be defended adequately in the very different domestic political environments of allies.

This is taken further because, in both Britain and the USA, expeditionary warfare does not enjoy automatic public approval. Shifts in public attitudes do not tend to command much attention in military studies, particularly if the military is a professionalized volunteer force; but these attitudes are important, even if their impact is dramatically lessened by the very indirect nature of democracy. For example, in Britain there will be scant public consultation about the decision to replace Trident, despite (or maybe because of) its great importance to defence policy. The same would be true if Britain took a role in the American missile defence system beyond what has already been agreed: upgrading Fylingdales radar station and using it for missile defence.

There have been complex shifts in attitudes toward expendability among young adult males. Modern societies depend on them relatively less than do muscle-based subsistence societies and, thanks to demographic growth, there are greater numbers of such males. On the other hand, smaller families have made every child precious, and the cult of youth is not a cult of organized violence. There is no equivalent to the child soldiers of parts of the Third World. Instead, there is an emphasis on hedonism and individual rights, neither of which is conducive to militarism or bellicosity. Instead, anti-war attitudes play a major role in literature. 'War' – i.e. now anti-war – poetry from the period of World War One came to play a major role in school syllabuses from the 1960s. This affected the attitudes of those who subsequently rose to power and influence, adding a wider cultural strain to the attitudes focused on opposition to atomic weaponry.

More generally, changing ideas of social order and masculinity were related to the rising influence of women and female stereotypes, and to the public perception of homosexuals. Women and homosexuals can, of course, be both bellicose and effective warriors, but the public does not associate them with those characteristics. Similarly, a decline in fatalism, along with a desire to eliminate risk, brought about a widespread reluctance in society to accept the hazards of warfare. As warfare became less frequent for Britain, and large-scale warfare ceased after the Korean War (1950–3), so it became less normal and normative. Instead, wars are increasingly perceived as aberrations, and this helps make them more controversial. A decline in society's bellicosity, and indeed its reduction to soccer hooliganism, may seem an ironic commentary on a state that is a thermo-nuclear power, a major arms trader, and an active participant in expeditionary warfare. It might be argued that Britain's military strength, both directly in its own terms and indirectly through alliance with the USA, is indeed a condition of the decline of militarism. However, in terms of public debate, there is no such harmonious relationship. Instead, there is a widespread unwillingness to accept the consequences of armed force. This creates problems for its use, as was shown most clearly in the controversy over the sinking of the *General Belgrano* in 1982 and in the debate over the extent of Iraqi weapons of mass destruction.

All alliances encounter upsets; for example, the relationship between the USA and Canada was, under the last Canadian government, in a far more parlous state than that between Britain and the USA is likely to be. The Anglo-American alliance indeed survived Suez, as well as the British refusal to support American interventions in Vietnam and Grenada. However, there are reasons to believe that the blow to the alliance arising from the Blair–Bush partnership will be more serious than any hitherto. This owes something to Iraq, but much more to the consequences of Britain's greater involvement in the EU and the degree to which the EU has not developed as Blair wanted. The Blair remedy of an outward-looking internationalism combined with modernization has not occurred. Instead, all Blair has to offer is the success in beginning the Turkish EU accession talks – a 'success' that may lead to yet further problems in terms of division within the EU, and that does not rest on an informed assessment of the national interest. At another level, concern about Turkish accession may well accentuate criticism of Britain and the USA within much of the EU. Given the drift of Britain's relations with the EU, this may make future cooperation between Britain and the USA more difficult. Yet again, military planners need to consider political constraints.

From this perspective, the reshaping of the military so that it can operate with American forces in expeditionary warfare is a response to particular political circumstances that are in keeping with Blair's reconceptualization of national interests away from the Cold War view of NATO and toward a wider interventionism that is designed to affirm the Anglo-American alliance, even as it relies upon it. Given the limited ability of British policymakers to influence American strategy, whether political or military, it is unclear that this shift is based on any critical assessment of national interest. Pro-Americanism is a reasonable approach, but it ought not to entail signing up for a role in particular military activities.

The same rule clearly applies to American support for Britain, but no one expects that this support would be offered other than in the context of American national interests, and this has been made very clear in the unilateral climate of neo-conservative writing in recent years. I was told by one such writer, Victor Hanson, that the USA would always provide support so that Britain and Israel could maintain their independence, but it was clear that the recipients were expected to give the USA unconditional backing in return. Those neo-conservatives who have been particularly active of late in the American policymaking debate doubtless mean well, but it cannot be argued that their apparently black-and-white view of the outside world has proved appropriate as a guide to policy, however effective it might be in public debate. Furthermore, the willingness to encourage a response to force is problematic. I was taken aback by one very prominent neo-conservative on 6 May 2005 when he asked me in conversation in Chicago whether I thought that Sudan could be 'taken out' by 10,000 troops. I replied that the capture of key positions in Khartoum would not lead to an end to resistance.

One wonders what role British forces are expected to take in such schemes. It is customary in Britain to be critical of the neo-conservatives, but there is a lack of appreciation of the extent to which Blair's assumptions are very similar, and Sir Christopher Meyer's account of his mission to Washington makes it clear that Blair shared Bush's views on Iraq. Blair's assumptions are based upon a notion of political redemption that is not one of compromise or nuance. At the same time, though, a hard-nosed policy of compromise has been attempted in the case of Libya, and in March 2004 this led Blair to visit Libya in order to meet Colonel Muammar Gaddafi.

Adopting a political or task-based approach to military commitments is the opposite of the capabilities-based approach conventionally used, and that accounts for the emphasis on transformation in Western military capability. While a task-based approach is the logical one, in the sense that there is little point preparing for what is unlikely to occur, there is the problem of the acceptance of risk and also the question of the accuracy of the intelligence and political analysis underlying the task-based approach. The issue of risk has been pushed to the fore with the question of weapons of mass destruction and the Iraq War. They both contrasted with the more contained commitments to the Balkans in the late 1990s. However, the sense of immediate threat conveyed by weapons of mass destruction is far from unprecedented. In terms of destructiveness, they are considerably weaker than the threats posed by atomic weaponry during the Cold War. The logic of deterrence suggested, though, that the latter would not be used, and clearly there is a difference now in the nihilism of Islamic fundamentalists. Furthermore, at the state level, the gerontocracy of the Soviet Union was more cautious than the rulers of Iraq or North Korea at the outset of the 2000s, which was just as well, as the USSR's capacity to inflict harm was far greater.

The task-based approach directs attention to the need to leave defence policy to politicians, with the military professionals providing advice on how best to tackle tasks, rather than defining those tasks. This is highlighted by the contrast between expeditionary warfare and a prospectus that does not call for such power projection. This contrast is one that underlies present issues on procurement, in that the government and the defence professionals are committed to, respectively, such warfare and the capacity for such projection, but there has been a less than full debate over either. Furthermore, the instinctual pro-defence ethos of Conservatives ensures that the party has played a very small role in querying the content or, far more important, the basis of defence policy. To talk of the military being under too much pressure and requiring more resources does not address fully the issue of the wisdom of the task, although this critique does indeed contribute to the discussion.

A direct engagement with tasking is difficult for the military, given the nature of civilian control and the resulting ethos. But ex-military and other commentators have a freer hand. For example, in *The Times* of 29 July 2002, retired Field Marshal Lord Bramall drew attention to the contrast between achieving military objectives and securing outcomes, citing 'a remark by a notably "hawkish General Gerald Templar" who when, during the Suez Crisis, Britain was planning a massive invasion of Egypt through Alexandria, said something to the effect of "Of course we can get to Cairo but what I want to know is, what the bloody hell do we do when we get there?"' This was very much the language of military prudence. In the shape of a wish for clear instructions, it became more necessary in late-imperial policing and post-imperial conflict, and was the British equivalent of the concern that, in the USA, led to the Powell Doctrine.

A desire for clear instructions is, in part, a response to the extent to which force is intended to achieve far more than the defeat of opponents. This has become a more pronounced feature of defence policy, as foreign policy has focused on a humanitarianism that requires a range of resources, both military and those of 'soft power'. This humanitarianism draws on the sentimental view of the outside world that leads, in particular, to a concern with those afflicted by disasters but, at the governmental level, it rests on a more hard-nosed attitude, in which the propagation both of positive views about Britain and of reforms to foreign systems are viewed as in the British interest. The last is a theme that is very much one of British policy today. It is argued that Britain is heavily dependent on distant lands, and that this is a matter not only of the traditional concern with trade but also of anxiety about national interests in terms of an agenda that includes the threats posed by terrorism, the drug industry, uncontrolled migration and large-scale crime. All of these are correctly perceived as a greater threat than during the Cold War and, as a result, defence priorities and policy have to address them. This may contrast with conventional assumptions about military objectives, but, in fact, these challenges invite a new form of threat-based planning.

At the same time, being a 'force for good', the goal proclaimed in the 2003 White Paper *Delivering Security in a Changing World*, is dangerously nebulous and a catch-all that says more about domestic positioning than the realistic prioritization of goals or discussion of force structures. Furthermore, the creation of a military capability to support this goal risks its being used. In a vicious cycle, such interventions may well make the world more difficult, and may directly challenge British interests. The extent to which Western interventions in Somalia, Haiti and Iraq did not end instability, but instead changed its form, is instructive. More serious is the inclination to press for intervention, both 'soft' and, if necessary, 'hard', in order to foster a process of political change in the Islamic world. However desirable the goal, the process risks associating political change with the West and focusing opposition accordingly. Speaking in April 2004 at the annual conference of the Society of Military History, Paul Wolfowitz stated that the history book that had influenced him most was Bernard Lewis's *The Emergence of Modern Turkey* (1961), with its account of the successful introduction of modernization in a Muslim country. In fact, this was a misleading comparison to use in the case of Iraq because, in Turkey, change was driven through by an internal force, the government of Kemal Atatürk – and the latter's legitimacy rested, in part, on defying the intervention of foreign powers. Indeed, that intervention helped forge the foundation myth of modern Turkey.

The Iraq intervention has highlighted the wider dimensions

of military activity. This poses a challenge for the British and, even more, for the Americans, whose doctrine had developed in the early 2000s in a process of transformation that sought to harness the latest technology to secure a major shift in capabilities and enable the effective pursuit of expeditionary goals. This, however, led to scant interest in stabilization, reconstruction and peace-support roles. Iraq highlighted the problem with this emphasis, and this has encouraged a rethinking of American views on transformation in which those roles have become more prominent. This more closely matches British assumptions than previously.

At the same time, whatever the goals, there are major problems with procurement. The launch of Smart Procurement in 1998 (later Smart Acquisition) has not ended the grave problems. Many of its principles have not been implemented, while, according to the National Audit Office, there are serious overspends and delivery delays in the demonstration and manufacture phase of projects. This hardly fosters optimism for the future, either with reference to specific projects or in terms of the knock-on consequences for the entire defence budget. Indeed, report after report by the National Audit Office has pointed out the serious problems arising from over-optimistic cost estimates, and this seems to be a matter not only of poor planning but also of the politics of project-pushing. This over-optimism seriously undermines the defence budget, as it entails an excessive burden of risk during the lifetime of a project. Linked to this is the problem of high inflation in the costs of procurement. As a result, the real increase in defence expenditure promised for 2004–7 could not prevent cuts. In fact, in some respects the increase was a consequence of the scale of the short-term cuts otherwise necessary to ensure a balancing of the accounts of the Ministry of Defence. Procurement is also designed to make cuts defensible by providing more powerful capabilities from fewer, but stronger and better-linked, platforms. However, issues of cost and delay suggest that this will be far harder to achieve than to suggest.

The 'spin' placed on cuts is, therefore, deeply problematic. In particular, the decision to cut infantry strength looks unwise and seems to be based on expectations of domestic stability that may be questionable.

CHAPTER 4

FUTURE SCENARIOS

Looking back at the future scenarios of the past, whether expressed in White Papers or by other processes of analysis and comment, it is striking how far the scenarios for what was then the future of the military focused on international goals, essentially in the shape of foreign threats. There was, by contrast, a marked tendency to neglect domestic challenges – apart, of course, from Northern Ireland. The domestic sphere was that of recruitment, not deployment. Understandable politically, as the British are sensitive about the deployment of troops on their streets, this was a less than open response to the range of capabilities expected of the military. Support for government, or civil control in a harsher light, encompassed not only an ability to overcome, or at least contain, labour disputes within a context in which some labour leaders had revolutionary inclinations, but also to help deal with civil emergencies and, not least, disaster relief.

Today, terrorism has made the domestic role of the armed forces even more important, but it has also diminished their role in its provision. This is because of the major expansion in the paramilitary function of the police, evident from its increased readiness – in armament, training and doctrine – to use firearms. The terrorist crisis of 2005 highlighted public sensitivity over this issue, but also a need for the police to be able to shoot on suspicion, however unfortunate the consequences might prove to be. The crisis also revealed the extent of the government's failure to overcome legal constraints on a robust response to terrorism, and the extent to which distrust of its policies affected much of the public and political reaction.

Looking to the future, it is likely that the military will have to adjust to the paramilitary role of other government agencies, in a new form of 'jointness'. At the same time, the nature of the 'domestic' sphere will alter greatly with the changing relationship of Britain within the European Union and the marked transformation of the latter. These issues are usually discussed in terms of the impact of the EU on external military activity and on procurement; but there are also important issues as far as the domestic dimension is concerned. The greater pretensions and extent of the EU present a number of problems both within Britain and in the expanding EU. Let us consider this. In order to meet its pretensions to power, and its ambitious policies of economic intervention, social welfare, and regional assistance, the EU is likely to have a high and aggressively redistributive burden of tax, both direct and indirect. In some (by then formerly) distinct countries, such as Britain, this will run counter to assumptions and past practices of low taxation. Furthermore, as a machine for redistribution, the EU will appear even more questionable, as the money will increasingly flow to Eastern Europe, or to Turkey if it joins the EU.

Yet there will be no effective way to change policy, or even express dissent, within the existing governmental or political process, and this is likely to bolster a sense of grievance and lead to widespread tax avoidance, and maybe pro-active obstruction along the lines of the 2000 British fuel protests. French practices of large-scale civil obstruction may also spread to Britain. It is easy to see how such processes could lead to violence. Government agencies will act as bailiffs, seizing property, and will mount intrusive surveillance operations that will, in response, lead to violence, quite possibly widespread. Furthermore, in addition to the citizen–government dimension, there may well be opposition between centrally controlled European agencies and their local counterparts and rivals, most obviously between European and 'regional' police forces. Whether the net effect is widespread local violence, or a full-blooded secessionist movement, the resulting situation will be difficult to contain. Thus, civil conflict may be seen as a consequence of the EU's lack of public support, and this will put popularly elected 'local' (currently national) governments in a particularly difficult position.

This may seem an implausible scenario in the short term, but is less so if the longer view is taken. It also serves as a reminder that the current approach to violence in the West – that it is a consequence of radical insurrectionary movements (such as the fundamentalist nihilism of Islamic terrorists) directed against the democratic state, and can therefore be readily treated as unacceptable by the bulk of the population – is not necessarily a guide for the future. It is clear that the vicious and dangerous threat posed by these terrorists has led to a tendency to present the Western state, governed as it is in accordance with an international legal framework and legitimated by democratic processes, as akin to a moral absolute. 'Would that this were so', might be the response of many, given the chaotic nature of the alternative, with its tendency – irrespective of ideology – to involve rule by the strongest. Such a dichotomy between a moral democratic state and chaotic opposition, indeed, apparently provides a safe intellectual harbour for the use of force, and thus an appropriate basis for British military doctrine.

The history of Europe over the last century, however, serves as a reminder of the difficulties of universalizing any basis for military doctrine; while the future trajectory of the EU serves as a trenchant warning that operating for a democratic and legal state may still prove a difficult basis for British military doctrine. The pretensions of jurists and courts are already driving this point home to British military leaders. The use of the law to challenge details of military activity stems largely from the incorporation of human rights legislation, which has been an aspect of British Europhilia. In 1998, British civil and European law were introduced to the military. The Human Rights Act was specifically applied to the military, which was expected to abide by the European Convention on Human Rights. The chain of command no longer convenes courts martial, and commanders, who have lost most of their disciplinary powers, do not review their findings. Furthermore, military personnel are subordinated to civil courts, the Crown Prosecution Service, and to related assumptions. The reopening in the civil courts of cases against members of the military that had been dismissed under the military justice system led to considerable disquiet in 2005, with the House of Lords debating the matter on 14 July. This looks toward likely difficulties over the projected Tri-Service Discipline Bill, which reflects a concern for judicial uniformity rather than military culture. The current use of the law pays scant heed to the problems of military activity and action, and has already led to public criticism from commanders, who find it a challenge both to their general duty of care to subordinates and to the culture and dynamic of the command hierarchy. For example, under the International Criminal Court Act of 2001, Colonel Jorge Mendonca was accused of committing a war crime because he did not prevent his troops from doing so: they allegedly assaulted detainees at a time when he was in no position to stop them. We have also seen the levelling of war crimes accusations against Colonel Tim Collins and the 1st Battalion, The Royal Irish Regiment in 2003, and the unsuccessful trials of soldiers in 2005.

These cases have clearly indicated a cultural clash between the nature of soldiering and the hostility felt towards it by many of the 1960s generation. So, even more clearly, did the legacy of Northern Ireland, with the long enquiry into Bloody Sunday followed by pressure to examine the entire practice of military operations during the Troubles. The fact that this quite patently failed to bring about an understanding of the difficulties faced by the military created anger and a more sustained disaffection, which had an impact on morale. It has also increasingly made recruitment and, more particularly, retention an area of major concern for the armed forces, as the required skills become more complex. The whole issue was further underlined by the pardons readily granted to terrorists as part of the Northern Ireland settlement, and their subsequent apotheosis within the political process. While it is reasonable to expect troops to conform to higher standards than the murderous thugs who comprised the terrorist groups of both sides, nevertheless the balance has been shifted not simply to suggest some spurious equivalence between the army and the terrorists, but even to pander to republican myths by implying that the army was, in some way, more culpable – in part because a small minority of those killed by the troops were not from the ranks of the thugs. This tension is worth considering, given the likely future positioning of the military within EU command structures, with their greater exposure to political direction and, in most cases, their limited understanding of the pressures of conflict. The use of unmanned military technology (though it actually requires quite a lot of manpower to operate and support) will scarcely solve the problem of the pressures of conflict and responsibility. This highlights the more general extent to which battle-winning weapons systems may not contribute as much as has been suggested to the range of military capabilities.

Conservatives and the military, both with their marked tendency to patriotism, will want to ignore the point about the acceptability of commands within an EU context. Nevertheless, it does need to be considered, if only in private, for otherwise the issue of appropriate obedience to legitimate authority, and thus of justified disobedience, will be left solely to the jurists. That is inappropriate, as the issue needs to be considered within a political context, rather than as part of some spuriously apolitical European judicial activism.

In strategic terms, there is the risk that European competition policies (and associated political horse trading) will lead to a situation in which key areas of procurement and maintenance are sourced abroad, with potentially serious implications for the reliability of provision – to say nothing of the British capability for independent action. Indeed, that capability is likely to disappear just as soon as resupply and repair become important issues. However, the British industrial base, even when assisted by key export markets, is inadequate to ensure long-term production capacity within Britain. This is particularly the case with high-tech weaponry, though less so with its lower-tech counterpart, such as hand-held firearms.

The problem of procurement is closely linked to alliance dynamics, something illustrated most famously by the Westland Affair of 1986: the fate of the company – acquisition by American or European companies – divided the Cabinet and led to the departure of Michael Heseltine, who had supported the European option against the wishes of Margaret Thatcher.

There are powerful political pressures for cooperation within the EU along the lines of the 2000 Letter of Intent framework and the later establishment of the European Capabilities Agency. The EU has an annual defence expenditure budget of about 200 billion euros, but the EU option poses difficulties in terms of shared political purpose. The American option is apparently even better at meeting procurement bills, but the ability of Britain to influence American policies through cooperation is limited.

Britain's openness to foreign sourcing of military equipment is in line with the pro-globalization policies of successive governments, but it does pose challenges to the domestic manufacturing base. (The flip side of the coin is the latter's inability consistently to provide *matériel* at the appropriate level.) There have been serious government failures in procurement, the most obvious recent example being the Eurofighter (a project that is dubious in conception as well as management), and such failures do encourage a resort to international competition, which offers an opportunity to enjoy lower prices thanks to the subsidization of production by foreign powers, as well as to benefit from the economies of scale created by an international market in which prime contractors operate on that scale because national markets are too small. The British manufacturing and knowledge base, while not fragile, has suffered from this readiness to turn to foreign suppliers as part of an international defence supply system. To maximize the fighting capabilities of defence without giving due attention to a strong and developing national defence industry is dangerous in the long term, whatever the savings in the short run. There are costs as well as benefits from imports, just as there are from exports.

All this may seem very abstract, but it is also within the sphere of current policy problems. International links create problems. If, for example, the EU lifts the embargo on arms sales to China, that will anger the Americans and jeopardize the EU–American military relationship, particularly in procurement, which, in turn, will hit Britain.

The EU and the USA could be complementary options for Britain. For example, the USA offers a supply of missiles that keeps the nuclear deterrent viable, whereas the EU cannot do so, not least because the British and French submarine-based systems are very different. The EU and the USA do not need to be alternatives, but there are serious policy problems in making them complementary. This problem is related to the viability of defence policy. Power projection entails capabilities that lead to relevant expenditure, but that also encourage a production base that may not be appropriate for more modest goals, or indeed be sustainable in the light of public expenditure requirements. At present the dockyards are benefiting greatly from naval orders, which is just as well, given the marked decline in merchant shipbuilding. In 1955, the UK was the world's biggest shipbuilder, but, whereas in 1962 its yards delivered 12.4 per cent of the ships that entered service, by 1983 the percentage was 3.5 and by 1992 just 1.2. By 2002, the only remaining merchant yards were in Belfast and Appledore and on the Clyde. Thanks to naval orders, however, in 2005 yards in Scotland, Cumbria and Southampton were building Type 45 destroyers (HMS *Daring* was launched from BAE Systems' Scotstoun shipyard in Glasgow in February 2006), and they will also play a key role in the carrier project. This was seen by the government as a welcome opportunity to move from the destructive boom–bust pattern of defence manufacturing. Indeed, in December 2005, Defence Secretary John Reid announced 'This project is a key to the defence industrial strategy and marks the end of the boom and bust industrial cycle. The introduction of a managed and steady work stream will allow industry to plan efficiently and to retain the shipbuilding in this country.' It is indeed possible that this policy will anchor the BAE company in Britain, and dissuade it from moving its centre of activities to the USA.

In political terms, there is the danger that European direction will lead to the use of the British military within Britain in a fashion that is unwelcome to sections of the military, or its leadership, and to a large swathe of the public – unlike during the Northern Ireland troubles, when military action was acceptable to most British domestic opinion. Viewed from the opposing Irish republican perspective during the Troubles, this future prospect would resemble an extrapolation of their view of the Northern Ireland situation onto a British scale. A number of political scenarios could be outlined, but it is also appropriate to consider the wider context of likely change over the next century. In place of the military's background domestic role during the Cold War, of action to cope with the calamitous consequences of nuclear war, come different modern scenarios.

These are generally seen in terms of the serious threat from terrorism, but it is also worth considering the environmental situation, both directly, in the shape of civil emergencies, and indirectly, in the impact on society. Both the emergencies and the impact will be felt most strongly in the Third World, and may directly contribute to the anger that provides a seedbed for anti-Western sentiments that are exploited to violent ends: both terrorism and insurgency. This is a more accurate (and troubling) way of considering the challenge from terrorism than simply conceiving of it as a top-down network that can be surgically destroyed.

Within the West, pressures from competing demands for resources will probably lead to crises of availability and an increased emphasis on government regulation. In some contexts, such regulation is only effective if it amounts, directly or indirectly, by edict or pricing policy, to prohibition, and this is very much in accordance with the regulatory tendency of modern government. Thus, concern about energy availability and environmental damage may lead to bans on the ownership or use of motor cars; to restrictions on the allocation of rooms deemed spare within individual dwellings; to water rationing, the prohibition of garden hoses, dishwashers or daily showers; and so on. However robustly they are defended on policy grounds as a mixture of conservation and fair allocation, and however well supported they are by political processes, such policies are likely to seem radical, disruptive, and an abuse.

The resulting challenge to these measures will have a largely political and legal focus; but the threshold leading to acts of collective obstruction, if not violence, may be reached quite rapidly in some spheres. A degree of regulation that might seem acceptable in wartime will not seem so in peacetime, however much the government may declare 'war' on nebulous targets, such as pollution, inequality, poverty, criminality, or drugs, as it is increasingly wont to do. Future declarations of 'war' may be aimed at shortages of water, housing, or other resource-based issues. The willingness to declare 'war' on domestic targets reflects a serious failure to understand the nature of war, not least the factor of risk and the likelihood of casualties. It also poses a challenge to the military in terms of mission creep.

Furthermore, looking to likely future state policies, the degree of regulation and control that was accepted or enforced during the world wars in Britain is now unacceptable to most, thanks, in large part, to democratization and the social changes of the late twentieth century. Such a prospectus may strike some readers as overly similar to the ramblings of Montana militiamen, but it is intended to underline the fact that anti-authoritarianism may well extend quite far. As a result, in the medium term, government policies from both the EU and London are likely to entail widespread policing that may well elicit a violent popular response, which the police will prove unable to counter or deter.

The military will not stand apart from this process. Instead, as the largest body of non-unionized, trained and vigorous people, at the service of the state and under central government control (unlike the police), the military is likely to find that it plays a major role, and one that is greater than the current doctrine of Military Assistance to the Civil Authorities. The run-down of the Army Reserve has ensured that regular troops will have to take the lead. The struggle to benefit from the state will become more acute as economic growth fails to occur at an overall rate that is capable of assuaging socio-economic demands, fears and expectations – not least concerning the basic adequate level of pensions. The consequences will have an impact on a weak government structure, on a system of public politics that is not attuned to a long-term crisis of this nature, and on a society where support for many of the consequences of modernization is limited, while opposition is often bitter. The result will be a search for government, collective and individual solutions that will only exacerbate insecurity, and provide excuses and occasions for violence.

An awareness of future domestic difficulties returns us to the point made by military commentators a century ago: that the health of the nation (in the widest sense) and its international strength are closely related. As a result, however constrained the bounds of military planning may be, defence preparedness, homeland security, or whatever other term is used affects the broad sweep of government policy. The military, indeed, is well aware of this through its exposure to social pressures and problems of recruitment. Thus, in the early 2000s, commanders referred to problems of physical fitness and attitudes toward authority.

At the strategic level, an aspect of the relationship between government policy and possible consequences for national vulnerability is provided by an energy policy that entails dependence on imports. Thanks to a decline in North Sea resources and to rising demand, Britain became a net importer of gas in 2004 and of oil in 2005. In 2020 it will be importing three-quarters of its energy needs. Imports lead to major concern over the stability of energy sources and routes, most obviously the Middle East, Algeria and Nigeria, stability meaning different things in these individual contexts. This concern does not have to entail force projection, but it does offer a geographical focus for the latter that has certain requirements in terms of force structure. For example, concern about the stability of routes implies a need to provide security for super-tankers both on the high seas and in choke points, such as the Straits of Hormuz and Malacca. A home-based strategy would supplement this effort by developing the civil nuclear sector, as well as renewable energy sources.

Another instance is provided by dependence on food imports. Over the last century, peacetime policies have clashed with wartime needs for food. In war, there were major and successful attempts to increase production, but the lead period was long: pasture land had to be ploughed up and seeded. In contrast, a future war will probably not involve any transition period, and instead there will be a vulnerability to supply routes. To argue that uneconomic domestic production should be kept going in order to provide a wartime margin would be implausible, given the costs involved (which are greater than the similar argument for multiple defence capabilities); but there is a key need for strategic reserves of foods and other commodities. At the same time, the just-in-time system of delivering goods to retail outlets creates real problems for any system of emergency provision. This is important in terms of responsiveness not only to international crises, but also with reference to potential breakdowns of domestic order.

Military leaders prefer to palm off such considerations onto civil policing, and this is accentuated by the tri-service command structures, where there is little place for either the navy or the air force in domestic control. Instead, their role in such structures encourages a focus on power projection. This, however, is a classic instance of the deficiencies of a capabilities-led approach, and one that was highlighted in the USA by the response to Hurricane Katrina in 2005: part of the Louisiana and Mississippi National Guard was in Iraq, and thus unable to provide assistance. Furthermore, although the nature and depth of the crisis owed nothing to the Iraq War, and was far more a product of the federal nature of policymaking, as well as of poor government decisions at federal, state and local levels, the trade-off between war abroad and failure at home was one that readily lent itself to public comment.

This, again, is a prospect facing Britain. The scenario of major deployment abroad and breakdown at home is not implausible. It may come as a result of military action in the shape of terrorist outrages, leading to calls for more troops on the street, or it may be due to serious problems with law and order, or to civil calamity. An instance of the second scenario is suggested by the rise of gun crime and the specific remark by the Chief Constable of Nottinghamshire that his force was unable to cope with the situation. In such contexts, citizens are entitled to wonder why money is being spent on the military if it is unable to help provide security. Arguing that force projection does so at a distance rests on the assumption that the domestic situation is reasonably stable, or that there is a relationship between confronting (or even creating) problems abroad and solving others at home. It may, for example, be the case that helping stabilize failed states will reduce pressure from illegal immigration, but that does not lessen the need to maintain a strong and flexible coastal patrol capability in order to deal with this, as well as with the entry of terrorists or drugs.

If violence does become a problem for Britain, particularly among communities with a sense of grievance, as already in Northern Ireland and deprived parts of British inner cities, the situation is likely to be worse in those parts of continental Europe where there is a much stronger tradition of political violence. This is particularly so in the Balkans, where the overlapping (but far from congruent) goals of nation building, resisting insurgency and enforcing peace create problems in defining and applying policy. Bosnia and Kosovo remain protectorates, each ruled by questionable governments, and it is unclear that this situation will change. Their stabilization is precarious, although they are certainly more stable than in the aftermath of the crisis of the 1990s. Some 50,000 troops were deployed in Kosovo in 1999, but by the start of 2005, only 17,500 were left. For Bosnia, the figures were 60,000 in December 1995 and 7,000 in December 2004. KFOR, however, is necessary to the precarious stability of Kosovo, while, in December 2004, the EU took over responsibility from NATO for security in Bosnia, EUFOR replacing SFOR. A similar transformation occurred in Macedonia in April 2003, although the military mission came to an end that December. Despite the problems of the former Yugoslavia, the pretensions and expansion of the EU have added, and will continue to add, an EU commitment to other parts of the Balkans. In December 2004, the EU took over the NATO mission in Bosnia. Furthermore, if Turkey joins the EU then its borders will march with Syria, Iraq and Iran.

The net result is that security issues within the EU will probably become a major call on the British military. Indeed, this is particularly so for the British military, because most other EU militaries lack comparable resources, professionalism and force projection capability, a point that was brought home by the failings of the Dutch force in Bosnia during the 1990s, and by the difficulty that the Spanish military experienced in fulfilling its political commitments for action in the first Gulf War. In the Balkans, there will be a major local EU player in the shape of Turkey. Its military is of considerable size, and this may well be a factor behind the EU accession talks, since this military will give the EU a greater capability. However, for religious and other reasons, it could be that a Turkish military presence is seen as overly contentious, most obviously (although not only) in the Balkans.

This will place the British military in a difficult position. Much of it may be expected, in such a scenario, to take part in *gendarmerie* duties that expose it to casualties in a more vicious and deadly version of Northern Ireland, the draw-down from which led the army to 'rebalance' away from infantry strength. This participation may be ordered by an EU government otherwise short of military assets and/or by a British ministry keen to gain advantages at the EU level by taking on an undue military burden, as both the Major and Blair governments arguably did. This certainly seemed to be a subtext in government policy in the 1990s and 2000s: 'punching above our weight' appeared to entail deployments and risks, in return for influence; or, looked at more harshly, trading lives for clout. This was certainly an aspect of policies in the Balkans, Iraq and Afghanistan. 'It were always thus' might be the response, but one way of approaching the future situation is to say that the degree to which troops will accept this may vary. In particular, the notion of loyalty to a country involving policing on behalf of the EU may be easy for politicians, but may test the professionalism of the military if it entails a long-term commitment, with neither end nor success in sight. From the Conservative viewpoint, the problem here is a political system without a sense of national interest, and thus the attenuation of patriotism. Patriotism is not an 'add-on' to military capability, but is instead a crucial contribution to morale.

The multiple failings of the EU will accentuate the problem. In both relative and absolute terms, many of the EU's key economies are failing. This poses a direct military challenge. First, the resulting crisis in public finances, and the more widely diffused sense of defeatism, will encourage a continued run-down of the military, as has been seen in Germany, Belgium, Spain and the Netherlands. This poses a serious challenge to Britain, not only in the shape of burden sharing within EU and indeed NATO operations, but also because the use of power by Britain will be viewed from the perspective of the non-militaristic values linked to the run-down of the military. A serious disjunction between foreign policy aspirations and defence policy exists at the heart of the modern European project.

Secondly, and arguably more seriously, the failure of key EU states to ensure economic growth sufficient to offset large-scale unemployment is linked to the radicalization of large numbers of the young, and this poses a major challenge to public order. Viewing the latter largely in terms of Islamic dissidence and terrorism, serious as these are, risks underrating the prospects of a wider crisis in public order, as was shown by the disturbances in France in late 2005. However, considering a crisis largely in terms of an international Islamic problem does leave a role for force projection and, hopefully, international resolution that is lacking if the focus is solely on the domestic situation.

Problems within Europe will cause grave difficulties for politicians and military planners. The prospect of chaos will challenge the suppositions of both. It was instructive to note the problems facing the French government in late 2005. Pressure to defend the republic in the face of a sustained challenge to law and order led to calls for the deployment of troops to support the police against the rioters, at the same time as there was widespread anxiety that this would further exacerbate the crisis. Though this fear was generally voiced by civilian commentators, it is certainly far from clear what troops can achieve that police, armed with stun guns and tear gas, cannot.

Commitments further afield will also cause serious problems. Here, Britain's ability to act is a function of the armed forces' capability (at last the navy and air force have a role), and also of the international context – specifically acceptance, indeed encouragement, by other major powers. This was seen with Suez, where American opposition led to the abandonment of the invasion, and, conversely, the Falklands, for which American acceptance, however reluctant, proved crucial. Since 1990, distant power projection by states other than the USA has only been possible if the latter is willing to encourage, or at least accept it, and that is likely to remain the case in the foreseeable future. Although great-power theorists write justifiably about the rise of a US–China rivalry, that is not likely to mean much outside Asia for some considerable time. Despite the large-scale development of its navy, a product of the major expansion of defence expenditure in the 1990s and early 2000s, China lacks the force projection the Soviet Union displayed at its peak. It therefore lacks a capability for, and a habit of, deterring actions by other states. As a result, British or French intervention in, say, Sierra Leone or Ivory Coast will continue to depend on American acceptance. The Chinese view is unlikely to be significant.

This, however, may not be the case in the Middle East. Greater Chinese interest in the region owes much to a wish to secure oil supplies, not least in the face of other powers' attempts to do the same in what has been called a modern Great Game. In addition, China sees the Middle East as a key area in which to build up influence. This is a major challenge to Western power projection, most obviously in the shape of the spread – direct or indirect – of military technology, including missiles and nuclear technology, to a number of hostile or potentially hostile states, such as Iran and Syria. At present, this challenge to Western power projection focuses on Iran. Western concern about nuclear proliferation entails the possibility of pressure, or even intervention (and indeed in 2005 the military expressed concern about the availability of Farsi speakers), but China is likely to be hostile to that step. The possible role of China adds an instructive dimension to current threat perceptions. The official website of MI6 declares that 'Regional instability, terrorism, the proliferation of weapons of mass destruction and narcotics are the major challenges of the 21st century.' Great-power confrontation is not mentioned.

Yet access to energy supplies will involve just such confrontation, while, more generally, the 1998 *Strategic Defence Review* declared that Britain 'must look beyond today's crises to provide insurance against the possibility, however remote it seems now, that Britain might once again face a major direct threat'. This provides the main logic for maintaining the nuclear deterrent, which offers a pre-emptive and retaliatory capability available to no other branch of the military.

The role of the military in guaranteeing energy supplies is likely to be one of the more important facets of the military history of the coming century. These supplies are significant in terms of strategic stability. For both the USA and China this involves a particular focus on South-West Asia, while Turkish accession will take the EU to the borders of Iran. In terms of this focus, the Indian Ocean becomes important as a strategic cornerstone for energy transits, and it will anyway become more significant as India's economy is set to become one of the top three in the world, while its population is projected to exceed that of China. The geopolitical importance of the Indian Ocean may well return attention to the potential role that Britain can take on as a naval power, although it is only likely to be effective in the face of opposition by a state (as opposed to, say, pirates) if this role is as part of a coalition.

The future nature of American policy, and the question of whether Britain will have any strategic leverage over it (and, if so, what kind), again returns the issue of British military policy to the political dimension. This is a dimension with which both major political parties are uncomfortable and unprepared, as it leads to a public discussion of contingencies that would expose the marked contrast between the politicians' desire to appear to dominate events, and the more intractable nature of circumstances, not least the compromises that circumstances force on moralizing. Labour has proved particularly weak in bringing forward this element, as it undercuts the moralistic tone of Blair's policies. However, this is not the full extent of the maladroit handling of military affairs under the Labour government. At the strategic level, mission creep has occurred without an adequate discussion of policy options and their consequences. These options were anyway constrained by the continued inability to manage procurement adequately, both in terms of costing and with reference to the failure to ditch arguably redundant, but politically convenient, commitments – such as the Eurofighter.

Furthermore, legal interventionism and the political direction of the military have both sapped morale, while uncertainty within the military and public unease about warmaking were encouraged by the Iraq War. In particular, the role of parliamentary scrutiny over policy, and the ability of government agencies, particularly the military, the diplomatic corps and the intelligence services, to generate policy advice without having it ignored or manipulated for political ends, are both unclear. The Blair ministry seriously squandered popular assumptions about the competence and integrity of government. The Conservatives' understandable desire to give no encouragement to Saddam Hussein or to radical left-wing opinion, and their unwillingness to reduce their support for the armed forces or for the American alliance, combined to ensure that they failed to offer adequate criticism.

As a result of the widespread reluctance to address the political dimension realistically, the discussion of contingencies by both major political parties (let alone the Liberal Democrats or the nationalists) is platitudinous, and there is a preference for emphasizing capabilities over assessing goals other than in the most superficial fashion. While understandable in political terms, this ensures that the public debate on military affairs is singularly weak. Indeed, it is becoming even weaker as neither party wishes to accept the consequences of Britain's failure to set the terms or even parameters of its relationship with either the EU or the USA. There is no sign that this will change.

Yet it needs to. It is difficult to avoid a sense of foreboding when one looks at a world in which environmental pressures are so severe. The likelihood that they will accentuate traditional disputes within and between states, and the possibility that new technology will not emerge as a genie to solve global needs for fuel, food and water, pose particular challenges. They may, indeed, lead to a medium term in which failed states become more common and their peoples (or at least a portion of them) a threat to others, whether through conflict, terrorism, forced immigration or other processes. This suggests that the burden on interventionism, and its military corollary of expeditionary warfare, may be far greater than is the case in the 2000s. It may also be that the USA is less able and/or less willing to bear the share of the burden it currently supports. As a result, the contemporary practice and doctrine of power may not be sustainable at the very time when, at least in terms of current paradigms, it becomes more necessary. Where this will leave the military is unclear. It may well be configured in the 2020s for a policy that was feasible in the 2000s but, however desirable, is no longer so. Alternatively, the policy, however desirable, may not be practical in domestic terms, because the political will to sustain the challenge is lacking, and in international terms because geopolitical competition will hinder the prospects for interventionism in failed states or against their rogue counterparts. This would represent a return to the situation of the Cold War, not with the same scale of global confrontation but rather with a plethora of regional challenges to the role of the hegemonic power (the USA) and its allies (including Britain). Nuclear proliferation will give some teeth to these challenges, but it is largely on account of their sheer number that they will be significant; and maybe also because there will be a relative shift of power away from the West. This will be felt most acutely by Europe, but it will also affect the USA.

Demographic growth and economic transformation – the latter not only through 'catch up' – will make South and East Asia relatively more important. Indeed, a 'benign' model of widely distributed growth will inherently reduce the role of the

West, however much it may benefit from its central role in globalization. A less optimistic scenario, in which growth is far less widely distributed, suggests not only areas of acute failure, such as the Horn of Africa or South-West Arabia, but also a mismatch elsewhere – for example, in India or especially Pakistan – between the availability of dangerous levels of military force and a failure to produce social benefits, such as widespread employment. This has been present in the 2000s, not least with oil-rich regimes such as Saddam's Iraq, but will probably become a more acute problem due to the difficulties of ensuring economic transformation.

This sounds like a case of more of the same for the future. But, although individual scenarios are likely to be similar, the general situation will probably be far more difficult. Britain's ability to respond depends on a realistic assessment of capability and a framing of goals in terms of a national interest that is sustainable because it enjoys public support. This does not mean no long-range missions, but rather strategic roles that are framed without being directed by the exigencies of particular alliance partners. This latter comment applies to both the EU and the USA. The British military needs to cooperate with both by drawing on a force package which is strong in particular roles that build on national expertise and needs. Commerce protection is an obvious example. In contrast, whatever the future requirement of allies, there is no need for a large-scale tank force capability, or for a large-scale aerial interception equivalent.

One of the themes of this essay is that a law-and-order capability is also necessary, however difficult that might be as an issue for political discussion. This remains the case, whether capability and power are to be discussed in their 'hard' aspects (the most common criteria employed in discussions of defence) or their 'soft' dimensions. The latter tend to be underrated. A domestic counterpart to a foreign threat did not occur during either world war, and if a domestic 'Fifth Column' was a factor during the Cold War, its activities were largely restricted to the already existing tradition of radical trade unionism. It is to the credit of Blair, scarcely the hero of this book, that he devoted considerable effort to trying to win soft support for British policy, both internationally and domestically.

This has become more serious – as both issue and approach – because of the attempts by Islamic fundamentalists to suggest a structural clash between Islam and the West. It is a view that both challenges Western power projection and raises serious questions about the extent to which substantial immigrant populations have been assimilated, at least to the extent of comprehending that opposition to government policy, or even social norms, ought not to lead to a violent reaction. The challenge is far more threatening if, instead of emanating from some hierarchical, centrally directed Al-Qa'ida (that could, in theory, be disrupted or destroyed by operations against its home base), the danger lurks in an amorphous agglomeration of autonomous local agencies.

The soft approach employs the rhetoric of universal concern, as when democracy is advocated for the Middle East. But when it is translated to the policy sphere, it needs to be defined more carefully in terms of the practical (domestically and internationally) than was perhaps the case in the early 2000s. There have, however, been valuable advances in the understanding of the extent to which military operations, however varied, are a part of a wider process in which many other agencies, British and foreign, play a role. Coordination is not easy, but advances have been made in some spheres. For example, the Ministry of Defence, the Foreign Office and the Department for International Development have established a pooled and shared conflict prevention budget. More could well be achieved in this sphere, but it should not be forgotten that the War on Terror relates as much to the domestic situation as to the foreign.

Whether in the use of soft or of hard power, the nature of the multinational operations in which Britain is likely to be involved will ensure that the options and perception of policy will be heavily affected by allied views and modalities. This adversely affected Britain in Bosnia, Kosovo and Iraq, creating operational sensitivities or difficulties for the military, and political problems for the government; but the situation is likely to be more serious if the support of allies is unavailable. The close-run nature of the Falklands War indicated this, and that was the case even though the USA provided important support, for example in logistics. A European response to a crisis in the absence of American support would be limited. This support is particularly necessary for satellite intelligence and airlift. Furthermore, given the relative failure of the European project, certainly in terms of growth rates to match those of the USA or eastern or southern China, the likely relative potency of European capability will diminish unless it is assisted by non-European powers. This may be a matter of positive support or of the very significant military-political role of non-interference; but, in the absence of these, it is difficult to see how European forces can do much beyond playing a role in a 'near Europe' that can be variously defined. If Russia was hostile and the USA disengaged, the definition would be very modest indeed, and would exclude Central Asia and the Caucasus. North Africa is an area of potential commitment, but again it is difficult to see what could be achieved in the absence of American backing.

This conclusion could be underscored by the experience of recent years. Sierra Leone, in which Britain made an important military intervention in 2000, was well within the capability for stand-alone offensive action, but elsewhere experience has been as part of a multinational force. This reflects the general problem of military capability in a context in which the power of individual states is unprecedented in terms of destructive force, and range and speed of action. At the same time, with the increased strength of most militaries, and with the obstructive role of armed irregulars, the ability to act offensively and to ensure success is limited across much of the world. This is especially the case given the importance of certain regional actors, for example Nigeria in West Africa. All this holds true even for highly professional and relatively well-funded militaries, such as those of Britain and France. The goal for these militaries of managing risk is far from easy, because it entails issues of preventative engagement and state-stabilization that are a world away from the prophylactic violence of a short-term expedition. It is difficult to see this situation altering, although the British fleet carrier policy may well suggest that, in certain circumstances, the parameters for possible action could be expanded.

Parameters will be defined ambitiously by military leaders keen to justify their forces and to play a role, and, even more, by politicians anxious to address problems and to play a role. Cooperation between these groups will be part of the floating international alliances that have become increasingly important since the end of the Cold War. In the new way of things, risks are particularly unfixed and both problems and situations are heavily dependent on perceptions. This has led to transient coalitions, as shared interests in particular missions are not matched by interests elsewhere. This position was not unfamiliar during the Cold War, but then there was a basic stability in alignments. Transient coalitions have become far more important subsequently, and the Iraq War was a powerful demonstration of the implications. Politicians and commentators tend to think of states as the building blocks in this analysis, with NGOs a characteristic of the unformed 'other'; but states themselves are coalitions of interests, and the relationship between military and politicians is one such. It is moderated, in particular, by Treasury oversight, as the 'group think' of the defence community does not lend itself to critical self-evaluation, and defence professionals seem to find it difficult not to parrot the request of the young Oliver Twist.

At present, although uneasy (largely on the side of the military), the relationship between military and politicians is working, because Blair's foreign policy provides a major role not just for the army, but for all three services. Whether the relationship would be as easy in a post-Blair Labour government is far from clear. The extent to which the relationship is overly determined by a particular foreign policy is another question. In conclusion, whether in opposition or in government, the Conservatives need to be aware of these issues, and of the extent to which the shifting coalition of government and military serves to constrain the former as well as the latter.

CHAPTER 5

CONCLUSIONS

The conclusions are fairly bleak, both for Britain and for the particular concerns of the Conservatives. On the plus side, there is the well-honed professionalism, dedication and can-do approach of the military, and the extent to which it enjoys a broad range of popular support. Indeed, in 2005, the anniversaries of Trafalgar and the end of the Second World War saw a positive popular and media response to Britain's military past and legacy – far more positive than would have been the case thirty or forty years ago.

The negatives, unfortunately, are more striking and immediate. In a situation at once welcome (the end of the Cold War) and difficult (the far greater role of Islamic fundamentalism), the military has been reconfigured away from a static, threats-based concept of national security, predicated on defence against a possible Soviet onslaught, toward a pro-active approach to a threats-based environment that is both very ambitious in its geographical range and worryingly ambiguous about the range and prioritization of the threats. So far, despite the difficulties of dealing with the aftermath of the overthrow of the Taliban and the Iraq invasion, there have been no disasters. Nevertheless, the strains of the expeditionary policy have already opened up serious questions about mission definition and creep; the extent to which it will enjoy sufficient domestic support in the future; related issues of homeland security; implications for military cooperation within the EU and with the USA; and, in the medium term, the extent to which rising costs will permit the military to retain a cutting-edge, tri-service, expeditionary capability at the operational level. All of these are important issues for the Conservatives. So, also, are those posed by growing judicial and political intervention in the workings of the military and, more generally, the incoherent government management of it, not least the strains that excessive operations put on readiness and the mismatch between future procurement promises and current financial pressures. There have been ample warnings about all these issues.

Yet it is far from obvious how the Conservatives can offer any more than ad hoc responses, unless they can define a clear-cut notion of the national interest and also present straightforward guidance as to what that means in policy terms. Neither has been particularly apparent. Indeed, from 1997, the succession of shadow secretaries of state – Sir George Young, John Maples, Iain Duncan Smith, Bernard Jenkin, Nicholas Soames, Michael Ancram, Liam Fox – is such that it has been difficult to build up continuity and experience at that level, although other members of the team have provided both. Labour, by contrast, has had only three secretaries of state for defence since 1997: George Robertson, Geoff Hoon, and, since 2005, John Reid. The contrast helps account for the difficulties the Conservatives have encountered in driving home political criticisms.

The definition of the national interest must address the relationship between homeland security and power projection by presenting them not as rival goals, but as twin needs, each of which has to be defined within the context of the practical. This latter, furthermore, cannot be defined away by simply saying that more money must be spent: the invariable resort of most defence politicians. Indeed, the profligate nature of national expenditure under Labour has seriously dissipated the sound financial inheritance left by the Conservatives in 1997 (in the USA, ironically, the Republicans have done the same to the Clinton legacy); and there is serious pressure for public expenditure cuts. This pressure will become worse as a result of structural features, including the ageing of the population (which will greatly increase the burdens of social welfare and state pensions), and the expansion of the European Union to include poor countries, which will lead to major redistributive pressures of a different nature. The EU rebate alone would purchase much equipment, and Blair's failure in December

2005 to use it to secure a more appropriate fiscal regime for the EU is a serious blow to the general capability of Britain as both state and society. In this context, it is difficult to see how defence expenditure will rise in real terms. Indeed, whatever the views of defence spokesmen, there will likewise be pressure in any Conservative government for cuts. At present, it is not clear how informed any related debate within government and party will be. There is scant room for optimism on this score.

Furthermore, there are contentious issues for any Conservative government over homeland security, entailing, in particular, the balance of security and civil liberties. This is not an easy balance to strike, and there is a danger that the travails and exigencies of office will lead the Conservatives to pursue authoritarian assumptions without necessarily enhancing security. In addition, power projection requires the pursuit of intervention within parameters that put a greater emphasis on clear goals, widely agreed backing, and time-limited deployment than has been characteristic of Labour policy under Blair. This is not so much a counsel of perfection as a reminder of the need for a clearer assessment of interests and risks than has been shown under Blair.

More generally, the Conservatives have to make an effort to draw together foreign and defence policies better than Labour has managed to do. They also need to ensure that the balancing of manpower and technological force multipliers, with all the long-term consequences, does not weaken the former for the sake of present-day expediencies.

Furthermore, there are the problems posed by the extent to which the Iraq War and the extensive debate over whether it was just and/or necessary have created uncertainty over the degree to which future expeditionary warfare (say a conflict with Iran) will gain legal authority and popular and political support. This is linked to tensions in the relationship of trust between civilian control and military command that the Iraq War caused, precipitated, or exposed, depending on one's point of view. Trust in government – not just this government, but any government – over issues of defence and security has been badly compromised; and the Conservatives need, if close to office, to move from criticizing the government on this score to considering the implications for any Conservative government. This will affect policy decisions. 'Trust us, we are not the last lot' will not work, however attractive that formulation may seem. The Conservatives need to rebuild a widespread willingness to endorse robust action, and, as David Cameron recently suggested, not simply rely on executive authority in the shape of the royal prerogative, however tempting that might be (and indeed necessary in some circumstances). Linked to this is the need to restore public confidence in the use and presentation of intelligence. Integrity is clearly a key issue, but can only be part of the solution.

The Iraq War also acted as a focus for disquiet over cooperation both within the EU and with the USA. The divided response of the EU ensured that the European Security and Defence Policy appeared less plausible, while in Britain political and military confidence in American military policy and implementation were challenged. The Conservatives, again, need to consider this. Bush's clear partiality for Blair extended to a disinclination to develop close links with Michael Howard. Putting aside the issue of personality, this underlined the fact that the Conservatives' support for the Iraq policy, far from yielding greater political access or influence, gravely compromised their ability to ask serious questions about the general thrust of British policy. At the same time, the lesson of late 2004 should be reiterated: American policy represents a range of options. This is particularly true of international relations, and it is likely that Bush's successor will reverse some of his priorities. The range of options is also true of military policy, and while this does offer Britain some possibilities, it also poses several problems. One such is the marked tendency of British politicians to exaggerate the strength of the 'special relationship'. The relationship is in no imminent danger of rupturing, but it cannot be taken for granted and must be handled with care. National self-interests may align but they do not coincide.

To organize the military in response to a particular set of American requirements would be unwise. Interoperability is a virtue, but should not be a goal that sets British priorities. Linked to this are issues of strategy and procurement. For example, Britain's commitment to a missile defence system would be costly and would represent a commitment to the American system that may be regarded as imprudent, since there will be real burdens without necessarily any ability to affect American policy. Good relations between the Ministry of Defence's Missile Defence Centre and the Missile Defense Agency of the American Department of Defense are largely irrelevant in the face of questions about the political value of such a commitment, let alone the impact of expenditure on the defence budget. British commentators need to be cautious about recommending policies to 'keep up with the Americans' that risk penury.

More central to British concerns is maintenance of the nuclear deterrent. Given that the first of the submarines needs replacing in about 2023, the main costs are likely to occur from 2015. Thus, any government elected in, say, 2009 will need to address this urgently, as the decision to assess a specific number of options, the 'Initial Gate' decision, will need to be taken that year. The relationship between the deterrent and missile defence needs to be considered, as the latter may be more effective against rogue states and terrorists, neither of which would employ conventional notions of risk assessment and cost-benefit analysis, such as those that underpinned deterrence theory. Even if missile defence is ineffective, deterrence is likely to be even more so. The argument that the deterrent is needed to underpin Britain's international position vis-à-vis the USA is unconvincing, and may be further undermined by America's greater need (political more than military) for the benefits of Britain's expeditionary posture. The Conservatives are likely to support the maintenance of the deterrent, but they need to consider not only the many options it entails, but also how best to present such a policy. There is a more general need to consider how to sell policies to an electorate that has changed socially and in its political assumptions, and defence cannot be dissociated from this.

If the nuclear deterrent is the key cost, there are other

important ones that the Conservatives must address. In particular, tranche three of the Eurofighter will be an issue in 2007. Hitherto, there has been agreement to take 55 planes in tranche one, and 89 in tranche two (the second order was signed in December 2004), but that leaves another 88. As yet, the government has not disclosed the cost if this purchase is not made, but there is a need for critical thought as to whether the money could be better spent elsewhere within the defence budget. This issue has been accentuated by serious delays and cost overruns with the Eurofighter.

As far as the navy is concerned, there is the question of the impact on other naval concerns of the investment, first, in the carriers and then in the upgraded nuclear deterrent. These represent formidable costs that will offer important possibilities for the power projection necessary to 'punch above our weight', the goal so dear to government of both parties. The original budget for the two 65,000-ton carriers was £2.9 billion, but by 2005 it had risen to a likely £3.6 billion. This, however, is a policy that is not without serious dangers. Investment in a small number of units, whether carriers or nuclear submarines, brings with it the hazard that any improvement in anti-ship or anti-submarine technology, whether of intelligence or of weaponry, raises serious concerns of vulnerability. These, of course, can be countered by defence systems against missiles or 'smart' mines or depth charges, but the difficulty of maintaining a capability gap in defence is considerable. Furthermore, the case of the USS *Cole* indicates another important aspect of vulnerability – one that carriers are particularly susceptible to.

There is also the issue of whether fleet carriers are an inherently obsolescent system. The carriers are not due for delivery until after 2013, and there is the possibility that force could by then be delivered by lighter-weight unmanned drones or submarine-fired cruise missiles, and that the capability of (manned) planes from distant airfields could be enhanced by mid-air refuelling.

Carriers are defended on the grounds that they are visible (and are thus an important element of diplomacy and, if necessary, intimidation) but 'over the horizon', and therefore far less vulnerable when it comes to occupying and controlling terrain. Both these aspects of the equation are correct; however, despite frequent assertion, the argument that they lead to a predictable and powerful impact is far less apparent. In the absence of naval opposition, such deployment may have only a limited impact on opponents who do not concern themselves greatly with the situation offshore. If such opposition is feared, as in the Falklands campaign of 1982 or the Armilla patrol, then the need to protect vessels becomes an important operational goal, with consequences that can reduce freedom of action.

Very different views are taken on the merits or otherwise of the carriers. The issue becomes more serious in the context of the overall defence budget and the possibly destabilizing implications of the current commitment to force projection. This commitment raises concerns not only about the state of the British military, but also about the envelopes in which it might be placed. Some of the focus has, of late, been on the problems of the coalition in Iraq, not least on differences between American methods of semi-warmaking and British notions of peacemaking. There is a fundamental difference between the British philosophy of minimum force and its American counterpart of overwhelming force, a route Britain could not afford to take.

Afghanistan, however, is a more potent instance of the weakness of power projection, because it draws attention to the problems of NATO and the difficulties it is encountering in overcoming them. NATO took over the International Security Assistance Force (ISAF) in 2003 but, although the size of the force has risen to about 10,000 troops, NATO has found it difficult to extend a strong presence outside Kabul. Much has been made of the role of Provincial Reconstruction Teams, but their success is questionable, and the key part is played by provincial warlords. The British have been prepared to meet the American goal of extending the NATO presence in the south, the zone of Taliban support, but this policy has been questioned by commentators, who are unsure of NATO's ability to discharge such a mission successfully. Other NATO powers, particularly France, are ready to see such a policy as essentially designed to support American objectives. Linked to this is the confusion of purpose between stabilization and counterinsurgency. NATO's presence in Afghanistan is an aberration driven by political calculation. Essentially a war-fighting organization, NATO has recently emphasized alliance transformation, but it is not set up to deliver post-conflict political and civil reconstruction, unlike both the UN and the EU.

These are not mere addendums. Instead, they raise important issues for British politicians as they struggle to define acceptable parameters for action. By the time of the next election, it ought to be clear whether NATO and EU goals can be realized. The impact of success or failure will be one that whatever government is elected in 2009 will have to address. Given that success or failure will define European power projection, and thus affect its British counterpart, it is necessary for British politicians to consider how best to address the issue. In particular, there are implications in terms of encouraging a reliance on alternatives in the shape of (large) American-led coalitions or (smaller) British-led ones, or indeed unilateral British action. The practicality of these operations in any given situation is a matter of some concern. If, for example, American forces are heavily committed in the politics of confrontation over South Korea or Taiwan, then, whatever their ambitions, the options for American-led coalitions elsewhere are limited, particularly if a sustained state-building role is involved. In this context, the feasibility of a British-led or British-only force may be limited, depending on the task and the likely opponent.

Furthermore, there is the issue of likely political consequences, not least the response of public opinion. If NATO, EU or, indeed, UN interventions are seen as normative, then the degree to which others will be deemed acceptable is likely to cause problems, not least in terms of a judicial culture driven by a particular conception of international norms. The Conservatives need to appreciate just how much the Iraq War has unsettled the situation. Here again, the assumptions of the past are of limited value. The CND years accustomed many

Conservatives to regard dissent over foreign and defence policy as something involving the 'usual suspects'; but the breadth of dissent over the Iraq War, and, in particular, the criticism from within the establishment about means rather than goals, have helped redefine the parameters of political reference. Governments, of course, can ignore these, but they need to be aware of the extent to which the arguments will play a major role in political debate and even more in the public responses ahead of an election.

To return to policy, the issue of force projection is central to current tasking. Current commitments are not adequately funded, but that is part of a more general situation in which the goals outlined in the *Strategic Defence Review* of 1998 were not adequately supported. Indeed, in some respects it was part of an all-too-common pattern of New Labour spin. The consequences were clearly voiced by Lord Boyce, a former Chief of the Defence Staff, in the House of Lords on 17 January 2005. He referred to 'significant cuts, now being taken in the front line' and 'the hollowing out that is going on', and levelled serious charges about the impact on service morale. Given that overall real defence expenditure is unlikely to rise substantially in future years, this obliges both government and opposition to address the issues of manpower/procurement trade-offs and excessive commitments. Hard choices; and it is all too easy to turn to the fudge, whether Labour spin about goals or Conservative calls for more money. Neither, unfortunately, offers much comfort in terms of an informed and grounded understanding of priorities. In part, the Conservatives need to decide whether they want a defence policy for opposition or for government. Given the current emphasis on not committing the party to spending before future fiscal circumstances are clear – in other words, not supplying Labour with ready hostages to fortune – it is likely that they will avoid getting to grips with defence costs for some time. In the meanwhile, there will be remarks aplenty about not endangering the country's security and national interests. Such comments, however, do not engage adequately with the issues.

SELECTED FURTHER READING

A. J. Bacevich and E. Imbar (eds), *The Gulf War of 1991 Reconsidered* (2003).

A. J. Bacevich and E. A. Cohen (eds), *War Over Kosovo: Politics and Strategy in a Global Age* (2002).

S. Biddle, *Afghanistan and the Future of Warfare: Implications for Army and Defense Policy* (2002).

B. Bond and M. Melvin (eds), *The Nature of Future Conflict: Implications for Force Development* (1998).

C. Coker, *Waging War Without Warriors? The Changing Culture of Military Conflict* (2002).

T. Collins, *Rules of Engagement: A Life in Conflict* (2005).

R. M. Connaughton, *Peacekeeping and Military Intervention* (1990).

A. H. Cordesman and A. R. Wagner, *The Lessons of Modern War. IV. The Gulf War* (1996).

I. H. Daalder and M. E. O'Hanlon, *Winning Ugly: NATO's War to Save Kosovo* (2000).

M. Duffy, T. Farrell and G. Sloan (eds), *European Defence in 2020* (1998).

R. English, *Armed Struggle: The History of the IRA* (2003).

A. Finland, *The Royal Navy in the Falklands and the Gulf War. Culture and Strategy* (2003).

L. Freedman, *The Revolution in Strategic Affairs* (1998).

L. Freedman, *The Official History of the Falklands Campaign* (2005).

C. Gray, *Strategy for Chaos: Revolutions in Military Affairs and the Evidence of History* (2002).

C. Gray, *Another Bloody Century: Future Warfare* (2005).

E. J. Grove, *Vanguard to Trident: British Naval Policy Since World War Two* (1987).

A. Hills, *Future War in Cities: Rethinking a Liberal Dilemma* (2004).

S. T. Hosmer, *The Conflict over Kosovo: Why Milosevic Decided to Settle When He Did* (2001).

T. Judah, *Kosovo: War and Revenge* (2000).

G. Keppel, *The War for Muslim Minds: Islam and the West* (2004).

B. S. Lambeth, *NATO's Air War for Kosovo: A Strategic and Operational Assessment* (2001).

C. Lord, *Intermediate Deployments: The Strategy and Doctrine of Peacekeeping-Type Operations* (1996).
J. Mackinlay, *Defeating Complex Insurgency. Beyond Iraq and Afghanistan* (2005).
M. Mader, *In Pursuit of Conceptual Excellence. The Evolution of British Military-Strategic Doctrine in the Post Cold-War Era 1989–2002* (2004).
P. Moorcraft, G. Winfield and J. Chisholm (eds), *Axis of Evil: The War on Terror* (2005).
R. Moore, *The Royal Navy and Nuclear Weapons* (2001).
P. Robinson, *Doing Less with Less: Making Britain More Secure* (2005).
G. D. Sheffield and G. Till (eds), *The Challenges of High Command. The British Experience* (2003).
S. Sloan, *NATO, the European Union and the Atlantic Community: the Transatlantic Bargain Reconsidered* (2003).
P. Smith (ed.), *Government and the Armed Forces in Britain, 1856–1990* (1996).
R. Smith, *The Utility of Force: The Art of War in the Modern World* (2005).
H. Strachan, *The Politics of the British Army* (1997).